DIĂMONDS

in California

REFERENCE USE ONLY

REVISED EDITION
by
MARY HILL

288686
NATUREGRAPH PUBLISHERS

HEALDSBURG, CALIFORNIA
95448

CONTENTS

	Page
Properties of diamonds	7
The carat	13
Prices of diamonds	16
Unnatural diamonds	19
Where to look for diamonds	31
California diamonds in placer	35
Amador County	39
Butte County	43
El Dorado County	45
Nevada County	50
Placer County	50
Plumas County	50
Stanislaus County	50
Tulare County	51
Tuolumne County	51
Other localities	51
California diamonds in lode	53
How to prospect	64
How to file a claim	67
Bibliography	69

My particular thanks to Elisabeth Egenhoff, of the California Division of Mines and Geology (retired), to Rudy Kopf of the U.S. Geological Survey, and to Alfred Rodia, of Portland, Oregon, for their interest and help in preparing this edition of **Diamonds in California.**

M.H.

PREFACE TO THE SECOND EDITION

Since the first edition of this book was published, week-end prospectors and geologists alike have sought for– and found– small diamonds in California.   None of the stones has been worth more than a few dollars, yet all have provided excitement and fun worth a great deal more.   In the Soviet Union, prospecting for diamonds has not been on a fun basis.   Spurred by the discovery of an alluvial diamond, the Soviets launched a concerted effort in the 1950s to locate bodies of diamond-bearing kimberlite within their own boundaries, in order to free themselves from dependence upon sources of diamond under Western control.

They were enormously successful.   By 1964 hundreds of kimberlite bodies had been discovered, and the Yakutia district of Siberia was producing an eighth of the world's diamonds.

In scientific knowledge, too, the Russians advanced.   Russian scientific literature on kimberlite – the host rock of diamonds – excluding popular and technological papers, amounts to more than 3000 pages – greater than the total of the rest of the world in all other languages.

Not that interest in kimberlite is abating elsewhere, although the motive may not always be the search for diamonds.   Kimberlite is a rare and unusual rock; one that may be an exceptional clue to the earth's own tumultuous history.   In 1964, the International Geological Congress organized a session on "Carbonatites, kimberlites and their minerals," which attracted speakers from throughout the world.   In the United States, a 1971 Penrose Geological Conference was held on the subject of kimberlites; it, too, convened specialists in kimberlites from diverse nations.

Surely our understanding of the genesis of diamond will be increased by this exchange of information and ideas.   Whether new diamond fields will be discovered remains to be seen.

Sacramento, 1971

PREFACE TO THE FIRST EDITION

The late nineteenth century saw a diamond rush to South Africa comparable in size, intensity, and drama to the Gold Rush of California. People the world over were reinfected by mining fever, including many Californians who had not yet recovered from the gold epidemic. Some decamped immediately for Africa; others stayed at home, to hunt in their own back yards. Here in California, though no paying mine was discovered, a considerable number of stones were found — kindling the excitement of miner and prospector throughout the State. Local newspaper reports of the time asserted that diamonds worth as much as $5,000 were recovered from the hydraulic gold mines of the Mother Lode. Although this figure was never verified, valuable diamonds continued to be found, and interest in them did not abate with the turn of the century. In 1906, the U.S. Diamond Mining Company was organized to explore what was thought to be a kimberlite pipe similar to the South African ones. Though no producing mine came of this venture, the attention of the California mining fraternity was directed seriously toward diamonds. The time was precisely right for such an enterprise. In January 1905, the Cullinan diamond, the world's largest, was found in South Africa. Its value was estimated as high as $75,000,000. With such a star to set their sights by, it is little wonder that California prospectors began to examine their own territory more carefully.

Today the story of the search for and recovery of those California diamonds lies buried in the files of newspapers and out-of-print scientific documents more than a century old. *Diamonds in California* tells that story — together with pertinent new information, for the benefit of mineral collectors. and prospectors who propose to hunt for diamonds in California.

PROPERTIES OF DIAMONDS

The romantic haze that has surrounded the diamond since first it became one of our treasured possessions has obscured its nature, its origin, its use, even its identification. One of the very best clues to its recognition, one that has been used throughout the centuries, is its hardness: diamond is the hardest substance known in nature. In 1820, Professor Friedrich Mohs devised a scale of hardness consisting of ten well-known minerals. By testing an unidentified mineral against those in the scale, one may obtain the relative hardness of the unknown, a quick and easy aid in identification. Mohs' scale, now in wide use, consists of the following minerals in order of their hardness: (1) talc; (2) gypsum; (3) calcite; (4) fluorite; (5) apatite; (6) orthoclase feldspar; (7) quartz; (8) topaz; (9) corundum; (10) diamond.

Diamond will scratch all minerals below it in the scale; corundum those minerals below it, but not diamond; apatite scratches those below it (fluorite, calcite, gypsum, and talc) but not those above (feldspar, quartz, topaz, corundum, and diamond).

The scale is not an absolute one; diamond is many times harder than corundum, yet calcite is very little harder than gypsum. Then, too, there are differences in the hardness of the diamonds themselves: a slight difference between stones, and a difference in the hardness of the same stone when tested in different directions.

In the field, if no hardness kit is available, a fingernail or knife blade may be used to test common minerals. In general, one's fingernail will scratch anything softer than calcite; a knife will scratch anything softer than feldspar. For testing gems, hardness pencil sets or wheels that have small bits of the harder minerals (feldspar through corundum) mounted in holders may be purchased. Hardness is a property that should be used in checking only uncut stones; a few scratches on a cut stone can mar forever its beauty.

DIAMOND CRYSTALS

OCTAHEDRON

DODECAHEDRON

Because diamond is so hard a substance, its hardness has often been confused with indestructibility. Actually, it is neither tough nor indestructible. In California, during the heyday of placer mining a stone which, judging from the description, must have been a nearly perfect diamond crystal, was washed into a sluice-box. The miners, suspecting its identity, decided to test it by placing it on an anvil and striking it with a sledge hammer. The crystal was broken into a thousand pieces, so the miners concluded that it had been quartz. Possibly some of them had been educated in the Latin classics, for Pliny, the first century Roman scientist, stated flatly that diamond could never be crushed, but would split hammers used in the attempt. Pliny could not very well have made the test himself, for the observations he made personally were accurate and astute.

Diamond, though hard, is extremely brittle, as the California miners, though they may not have realized it, proved. It is this property that allows diamond to be chipped into light-refracting facets that give fire and brilliance. Its natural crystal form, when perfect, is most commonly the octahedron (an eight-sided crystal composed of triangles) or dodecahedron (a twelve-sided crystal composed of rhombs). Most diamonds in the rough state have a coating that masks their transparency, and their fire is brought out only by cutting. In the fifteenth century, Ludwig van Berquem of Flanders discovered the advantage of placing facets on the diamond to enhance its fire. He cleaved the stone, as gem cutters do today, by making use of its brittleness, perfect cleavage, and hardness. The hardness varies slightly with the crystallographic direction in the stone: most crystalline diamonds are harder parallel to the octahedral faces and less hard parallel to the dodecahedral faces. The cleavage, perfect parallel to the octahedral faces, enables the stonecutter to obtain smooth, clean facets with a minimum of waste.

Although van Berquem may have been the first to cut stones in the modern fashion — that is, to increase the fire— he was not the first to

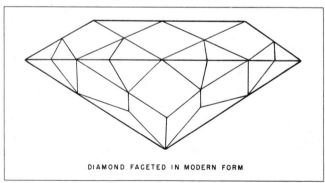

DIAMOND FACETED IN MODERN FORM

face the problem of faceting. In ancient times diamonds were worn almost as they were found; later, lapidaries in India contrived to polish the natural faces and to add small facets to conceal flaws. Lapidaries of ancient times and the Middle Ages, faced with the problem of trimming the stone, found the solution with difficulty. Diamond is so hard, they reasoned, that it will destroy hammers. (Pliny, whose authority was unquestioned, said so.) Something, therefore, had to be found to soften the gem during cutting. Their solution was warm goat's blood, which was supposed to render the stone reasonably pliable.

Diamonds are not particularly heavy, when compared with metallic minerals (their specific gravity ranges from 3.15 to 3.53, but commonly is 3.52 in well-crystallized stones), and not outstandingly heavy when compared with other gems. Quartz, with which they are most easily confused, is somewhat less heavy (2.66). Diamonds may be most accurately identified by their index of refraction, an optical property that can best be determined by the aid of a microscope or refractometer. It is this optical property, refraction, combined with another, dispersion, that allows diamond to show fire when properly cut. The index of refraction is a measure of the amount that light rays are bent upon entering a transparent or translucent substance. On entering a diamond through the top crystal face, the light rays are bent toward another crystal face, then toward another, reflected off yet another, and so on, until they emerge again as light from the top of the stone.

The fire or flash of color that accompanies the emergence of the light is due to dispersion. As is well known, white light is made up of the colors of the rainbow. Prisms of many substances will separate light so that the rainbow effect can be seen. In diamond, the many facets act as tiny prisms, and as light enters the stone and is bent— refracted— and reflected, the rays at the violet end of the spectrum are bent slightly more than those at the red end. The result is bright flashes of color and light from the stone.

It is now known that some diamonds will fluoresce or phosphoresce when exposed to ultraviolet, cathode, and x-rays, or to radioactive emanations. These properties are of particular value: x-rays may now be employed to distinguish paste or glass stones from real diamonds, as the diamonds are transparent to x-rays but the imitations are not. Some California diamonds are gray-blue under short-wave fluorescent light.

As is true of diamonds exposed to ultraviolet rays, sunlight also affects some gems, causing them to show a light-blue luminescence, or to glow in the dark with a greenish or yellowish color. The late Dr. George F. Kunz, America's outstanding gem authority during his lifetime, experimented with some 13,000 diamonds to discover their luminescent and phosphorescent properties. It was his conclusion that only certain diamonds – chiefly Brazilian stones – had the power of absorbing sunlight or artificial light and releasing it in the dark. All of the stones contained some foreign matter that made the phenomenon possible; the property is not inherent in the diamond in its absolutely pure state. Dr. Kunz named the unknown impurity "tiffanyite" in honor of Charles L. Tiffany, founder of the firm of Tiffany and Company.

This peculiar ability of stones to glow in the dark gave rise to many strange and wondrous beliefs in ancient times. Such gems were objects of fear, supposedly having the ability to cause shipwreck, to annihilate schools of fish, and to cast evil spells. Some sort of luminescent stone may well have been the original "evil eye."

Another property of diamond that has contributed extensively to its folk-lore is its poor conductivity of heat, which makes it cold to the touch. Diamonds were once used extensively – that is, by those who could afford them – as specifics for various diseases and as amulets supposedly containing remarkable curative powers. According to ancient prescriptions, only the best diamonds could be used, as poorer ones, instead of curing disease, would cause lameness, blindness, pleurisy, and leprosy. To cure ailments by external

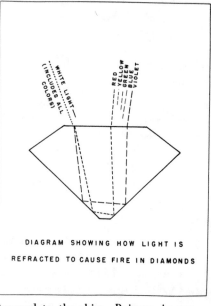

DIAGRAM SHOWING HOW LIGHT IS REFRACTED TO CAUSE FIRE IN DIAMONDS

application, the diamond was strapped to the skin. Poisons, in particular, were supposed to be exuded from the body and collected on the stone. The belief did have some basis in fact: rich persons who

CHARACTERISTICS OF DIAMOND

CRYSTALLOGRAPHY

Isometric (cubic system)
Octahedral form common
Dodecahedral form common
Twinning common, twin plane (111)
Variety "bort" consists of rounded
    forms with confused crystalline
    structure

PHYSICAL PROPERTIES

Cleavage perfect parallel (111)
    (octahedral)
Fracture conchoidal
Brittle
Hardness 10 (varies slightly with crys-
    tal direction)
Specific gravity 3.15 to 3.53 in crys-
    tals
Luster adamantine to greasy
White or colorless; very pale shades
    of yellow, orange, red, green,
    blue, and brown; variety "car-
    bonado" is black
Generally transparent; may be trans-
    lucent or opaque

OPTICAL PROPERTIES

Isotropic
Index of refraction, n = 2.42
Dispersion 0.063
No birefringence
No pleochroism
Transparent to x-rays
Some crystals fluoresce or phosphor-
    esce
Some crystals show anomalous double
    refraction

CHEMICAL PROPERTIES

Composition carbon (C)
Not attacked by acids
Will burn to carbon dioxide in oxy-
    gen atmosphere at very high tem-
    perature

SIZE
Microscopic to more than 3,000 carats

MAY BE CONFUSED WITH

Zircon, cassiterite, rutile, demantoid, hematite, sphene, beryl, topaz, quartz,
axinite, doublets, triplets, paste, glass, YAG (yttrium aluminum garnet)

could afford diamonds were, in general, less frequently ill than were poorer ones — probably the result of better living conditions.

Though the ancient and medieval writers had no very accurate idea of the true nature of diamonds, they did have a few definite notions about them. They thought that diamonds were the product of lightning flashes; that there were male and female stones, which could mate and give birth to smaller ones; that diamond dust was a deadly poison, yet that a good quality diamond could cure illness; that diamond was indestructible, yet that it could be consumed in a hot enough flame. One Hindu prescription for using diamonds to cure disease is provided by Dr. Kunz in his book *The Curious Lore of Precious Stones.* On an auspicious day, the Hindu physician took a diamond, dipped it in the juice of kantakara, and placed it in the heat of a fire made from cow or buffalo dung. In the morning, it was dipped in another solution, and again it was burned. This procedure was repeated for seven days to purify the stone. At the end of that time, the stone was buried in a seed paste mixed with asafoetida and rock salt. It was then heated twenty-one times, to reduce to ashes. The ashes were dissolved in a liquid, and the concoction imbibed to "conduce longevity, general development of the body, strength, energy, beauty of complexion, and happiness".

The idea that small quantities of diamond dust were lethal prevailed for many hundreds of years. As late as the sixteenth century, Benvenuto Cellini, the world-renowned goldsmith, was nearly poisoned by diamond dust — or so he stated. The only thing that saved him, according to his own account, was that the jeweler who was hired to grind the diamond to dust was poor but dishonest, and substituted a piece of quartz. In spite of this widespread belief, miners of the time swallowed diamonds as a means of stealing them.

THE CARAT

Probably nothing is more confusing in the study of gem stones than the use of the term "carat". Precious stones and precious metals have always been treated as things apart — substances not to be measured with the same rulers and scales that are used for baser things. The result has been near-chaos; fortunately, some semblance of order has been restored, though the subject is far from clear. The precious gems themselves are not weighed in ounces and pounds, or grams and kilograms, but in carats and grains. The carat has had a standard weight only in this century; the grain is still somewhat confused. There are "diamond grains" and "carat grains", "pearl grains", "troy grains", and "avoirdupois grains." The precious metals in which most stones are set – silver, gold, and platinum – are, in turn, not weighed in avoirdupois ounces, of which there are sixteen to the pound, but in troy ounces, of which there are twelve to the pound.

Sometimes, possibly to make a stone sound larger, the "point system" of measuring is used. Each point is one one-hundredth of a carat, so that a "fifty-two point" stone is only a hair's weight over half a carat. Each point, by actual weight, is only two one-thousandths of a gram. It would require about nine hundred thousand points of diamonds to balance a pound of butter.

To add another factor to the semantic maze, the precious metals are also measured in carats, after being refined. Nowadays the term is usually spelled "karat" when used for gold, to distinguish it from "carat" to be used for precious stones. Pure gold is "24-karat", generally marked "24K", but it is seldom used in jewelry; it is too soft, and therefore must be alloyed with other metals. The alloy added to the gold reduces the fineness: a ring marked "18K" consists of eighteen parts of gold to six parts of alloy.

The term "carat", as used in measuring the weight of precious stones, takes its origin from certain seeds used in Greek and Roman times. The seeds used by the Greeks – the locust-bean or St. John's bread – were taken from the carob or locust tree, the *Ceratonia siliqua*. These seeds were remarkably constant in weight, being usually about three-sixteenths of an English grain. In India, the grain used was a brilliant, glossy, scarlet and black seed from the *Abrus precatorius* weighing about two English grains. England, having no locust beans to use as weights, measured the English "grain", against a grain of "corne or wheate, drie, and gathered out of the middle of the eare". To add to the confusion, what was "corn" to an Englishman was not "corn" to an American. In England alone, six different kinds of carats were in use at one time. Nor was the weight of the carat in other countries at all steady: Florentine and Viennese weights have been historically irregular, and Indian weights no doubt varied widely. There is evidence, too, that some of the variations were deliberate.

WHAT THE CARAT ONCE WEIGHED AROUND THE WORLD	
Turin	0.2135 gram
Persia	0.2095 gram
Venice	0.2071 gram
Austro-Hungary	0.2061 gram
France	0.2059 gram
Portugal and Brazil	0.2058 gram
Germany	0.2055 gram
England and British India	0.2053 gram
Holland and Russia	0.2051 gram
Turkey	0.2005 gram
Spain	0.1999 gram
Java and Borneo	0.1969 gram
Florence	0.1965 gram
Arabia	0.1944 gram
Egypt	0.1917 gram
Bologna	0.1886 gram

With such international and intranational disagreement, it was apparent to reputable merchants and jewelers that some uniform system must be established. In 1871, a syndicate of Parisian jewelers suggested 0.205 gram as a good weight to be adopted internationally, but the suggestion was not universally accepted. It has been only in this century that the current value of the carat has attained world-wide use. In 1907, at the meeting of the International Committee of Weights and Measures, a value of 0.200 gram, or one-fifth of a gram, was recommended. Most countries soon adopted it; the United States agreed to it in 1913, and Great Britain, the last to fall in line, made it – the metric carat – the legal weight in 1913.

In this respect, at least, the slogan "let the buyer beware" has lost some of its meaning. Nowadays wherever a diamond is weighed, a carat is a carat at one-fifth of a gram.

The diamond fields of South Africa, 1869

PRICES OF DIAMONDS

Diamond, in company with other precious stones, has no unit value. Though all gem diamonds except the very large ones are sold by the carat, there is no set price per carat, as each diamond is a separate marketing problem. In general, a diamond is sold for whatever the market will bear: the size, purity, and rarity of color being the chief determining factors. In cut stones, the quality of the cut or "make" also affects the price.

As the gems come in many colors, including pink, blue, yellow, green, brown, red, and white, and in many grades, from badly fractured ones to perfectly formed crystals, some rough method of grading must be used.

For many years, a system of color classification that combined source and color was followed. It was rough, but served as a general gauge and protected in some measure both merchant and customer. The grades were Rivers, Top Wesseltons, Wesseltons, Top Crystals, Crystals, Top Capes, Capes, and Yellows. The term "Jager" was not included in the list, though it was applied to exceptionally high-priced colorless diamonds that had a bluish tinge in sunlight, or, more rarely, were actually bluish in body. The familiar "blue-white" of diamond advertising included the Jagers as well as the Rivers and Top Wesseltons; some dealers labeled Wesseltons and Top Crystals "blue-white" as well. In fact, almost any diamond that is not definitely some other color may be called blue-white.

In 1941, a diamond colorimeter was constructed that measured twelve divisions between yellow and colorless. By using this machine, key sets of stones were graded for sale to jewelers. Any diamond could then be compared with diamonds from the key set to determine its precise color grade. Although this was somewhat easier and more dependable than the older color designation that varied from merchant to merchant and depended partly on inducing a kind of hypnosis in the customer, the new color grades were difficult to determine unless physical conditions were exactly right. Reflections of all sorts may change the aspect of a stone — a fine day may perk up a diamond examined outside by showing the blue of the sky rather than the color of the gem; or the reflection of yellow or brown store fixtures can change the appearance of a fine colorless stone to a poor yellow. To avoid the disguising influence of sunshine, rain, dust, furniture, paint, or electricity, many reputable jewelers are using the "diamolite"–a diamond-grading unit specially constructed to prevent contaminating reflection. It is a small box that contains an artificial light filtered through a daylight blue filter. The filter system and light-diffusing interior make it possible to see the exact color of the body of a diamond.

About 1592 the famous Dutch traveller Linschoten formulated the "rule of squares" that for many years was a good quick method of obtaining a rough estimate of the market value of a precious stone. It states that the value increases directly with the square of the weight: a one-carat ruby of a sufficiently good quality to command a price of $1,000 on today's market would, if it were a two-carat stone of the same quality, be worth about $4,000; if a three-carat stone, $9,000.

The rule of squares is still valid for emeralds and rubies, but since the prolific South African diamond mines have been discovered, it has not applied to diamonds. Today, the value of a three-carat stone may be about twice that of a one-carat stone of the same quality; a five-carat stone might be worth three times the one-carat stone, and a twenty-carat stone five times the one-carat stone. In January 1959, the De Beers Consolidated Mines, Ltd., advertised the following prices as a rough guide for prospective purchasers: a quarter-carat stone, $75 to $240; one-half carat, $150 to $545; one carat, $540 to $2,000; two carats, $1,150 to $3,800; depending upon color, clarity, cut, and purity. Very large diamonds or very unusual ones are valued like works of art: the price is whatever the customer will pay.

Harry Winston, independent gem dealer of New York City, once purchased the famous Jonker diamond. Originally a giant stone of 726 carats, it was sold uncut for 75,000 pounds sterling. After being cut to one large stone of about 140 carats and eleven smaller ones, then recut to a 126-carat beauty, the diamond was still so large that it was very difficult to sell. Winston, in company with other gem dealers and traders who make their livelihood by buying and selling, prefers smaller gems that someone can afford.

"Keeping one [as large as the 126-carat Jonker] was risky," the New Yorker Magazine quoted him as saying, "I priced it at a million dollars, and it took me fourteen years to sell it. In the end, it took a king – Farouk of Egypt – to buy it. That's why I wanted the Jonker cut up in the first place. If I'd kept it as a single stone, it would have turned out to   be a four-hundred-carat one, impossible to sell at its true value. A million dollars is about as high a price as you can ask for a diamond."

Dreams of a diamond swindler. From *Underground,*
by Thomas W. Knox, 1873

UNNATURAL DIAMONDS

The prospector can encounter in the field many natural minerals that may, in the trade, go under such names as "Alpine diamond", "Alaska diamond", and the like. Most of them will be quartz or other minerals not to be confused with true diamond.

He will never encounter paste diamonds, or composite stones, unless his claim has been salted, as these are manufactured products not found in nature. Probably he will not find synthetic stones, even as salting, as the production of such diamonds has been too small to date to provide many stones for the underworld market— as far as any honest man knows.

Salted diamond claims are not unknown, although there is no record of imitation or composite stones having been used. Partly cut gems were used, though, in 1871 in one of the most remarkable swindles in history.

The story is really a California one, even though the "mine" was located in the Green River country near the boundary of Colorado and Wyoming and some of the action took place in New York and London. Briefly, it is this:

Two itinerant prospectors, Philip Arnold and John Slack, brought bags of diamonds they claimed to have found in Wyoming to the Bank of California in San Francisco for safe keeping. Word of their find spread rapidly, and soon they were being urged to permit investors to assist them with the development of their bonanza. At first Arnold and Slack seemed reluctant to accept any help, financial or otherwise. After considerable harangue, they agreed to receive investors and to lead a selected few to the mine. The bargain was struck, and some of San Francisco's most prominent men, including General George S. Dodge, proceeded to the secret location. Henry Janin, a well-known mining engineer engaged to examine the property, accompanied them. The entire party was blindfolded for the last days of the trip.

That the mine was indeed a rich one was apparent at once: rough diamonds, rubies, emeralds — all were scattered profusely over the ground. Small glittering piles resembling ant hills were encrusted with diamond dust. The engineer's report was a glowing one. Arnold and

Slack sold their interest "reluctantly" for a total of $660,000, and a mining company was formed at once to exploit the deposit. Capitalization was set at $10,000,000, and investors, among them some of the world's most astute business men, including William C. Ralston, Thomas S. Selby, and Baron von Rothschild, were invited to participate.

The exact nature of the "great diamond hoax" did not become apparent until Clarence King, at the time a U.S. Government geologist, visited the property during the height of the speculation. According to one version of the story, his companion, an elderly German, was entranced with such a fabulous place, where precious gems were to be had for the stooping. Both he and King were appalled when the German found one that was partly polished. King telegraphed the company at once that the mines were salted, and the great diamond bubble burst.

Neither the engineer nor other members of the original inspection party had been at all skeptical when they found diamonds, rubies, and sapphires in geologic affinity. "Why a few pearls," Asbury Harpending, one of the chief investor-promoters, wrote bitterly in retrospect, "weren't thrown in for good luck I have never yet been able to tell." He denied that the diamonds were ever found in the forks of trees, a story current after the hoax was discovered, but did aver that he recalled hearing a train in the distance. It was his opinion that, though the

One of the diamonds used to salt mines of the "great diamond hoax"

Abbreviations on the map are: N. S., Navajo Springs; Z. V., Zuni Villages; J. W., Jacobs Wells; M. W., Martin Well; J. D. M., Jornadin del Muerto; C. w. I., Cliff with Inscription, Spanish, dated 1708; D. B. o. R., Dry Bed of Old River; B.C., Bear Camp; I. H. o. A., Immense Herds of Antelopes.

Shown above is a map of the "Diamond Fields" of western United States, drawn in 1872. Although the fields were supposed to be located east of California, most of the story took place in San Francisco and London as the claims were active on the market (no less than seven companies were organized to mine them), but not at the location. A great many diamonds were picked up on the claims - all planted - but none was ever mined. The fields were said to be located in Arizona, but later "experts" pronounced them to be in New Mexico Territory, as may be readily seen by the immense ant hills and other diamantiferous deposits shown here. At one point in the excitement (hardly anybody had been to the claims, and most of the people who had gone had been blindfolded), ex-Governor William Gilpin of Colorado announced that they were in the San Juan Mountains of his territory. He had, he said, seen many emeralds and other precious stones from there, which he described in such glowing terms that editors quoting him conceded that it must surely be a "new El Dorado". In Africa, where the initial excitement of the diamond rush was dying out, restless prospectors heard the news of the Arizona strike and headed for America. Nobody, whether African or native, had the slightest idea where to go to find the "fields", though many went. Some sent samples back from Salt Lake, supposedly containing diamonds discovered near the Uinta Mountains; others said the fields were 150 miles from Cheyenne. Wherever they were, "it is satisfactory to know they are located somewhere," concluded the somewhat skeptical writer in *Mining and Scientific Press.* Unfortunately, they weren't.

horseback portion of the trip had occupied four gruelling days over rugged country, they were never more than twenty miles from the railroad.

One of the rough diamonds used to salt the mine is now on display at the California Division of Mines and Geology in the Ferry Building in San Francisco, but probably quite a few of the diamonds that were used as "salt" are still in the western wilderness. It subsequently was discovered that Arnold and Slack paid some $25,000 for the considerable number of second-rate diamonds they so lavishly spread about their "mine". Some of these stones, of course, they carried with them to San Francisco as exhibits (they were erroneously valued by Tiffany's at $150,000.)

On today's market, several natural stones are used to imitate diamonds. Among these are quartz, zircon, corundum, calcite, topaz, and beryl. All of them can be easily identified by their optical properties (all have two indices of refraction) and most certainly by their inferior hardness. None approaches the hardness of diamond; diamond is eighty-five times as hard as corundum, which stands next to it in the Mohs hardness scale. The amateur gemologist will do well to avoid the hardness test, however, in cut stones, as he may damage a soft stone or break a tiny brittle cutlet on the bottom of a true diamond.

Among the artificial stones, the most common diamond imitation is made of a "strass" or lead glass, also called "paste". It is commonly used in rhinestone jewelry, in which the small stones are known as "brilliants"— to be distinguished from brilliant - cut diamonds. Most of the brilliants are backed by metal foils or coatings of mercury or metallic pigment.

One formula for making strass calls for one part of crushed quartz and three parts of cream of tartar, melted together in a crucible. Pour into lukewarm water, add nitric acid as long as it will boil. Dry the mixture, and add one and one-half parts of white lead. Take one and one-half parts of the mixture, add one-twelfth part of borax, melt, and cool by pouring directly from the crucible into cold water. Add one-twelfth part of saltpeter and melt. As it requires extremely high temperatures to melt the quartz in the initial step — about 573 degrees centigrade—this is not a good recipe to try on the kitchen stove.

Most stones that are used as diamond imitations are not polished by the same methods as diamond, and will not show the characteristic flat faces. An exception to this is zircon, which was commonly cut in

Bangkok, where the same techniques used in faceting diamonds were used. Recently, an artificial stone called "YAG" has been placed on the market and advertised widely. It was named for its mineral composition, yttrium aluminum garnet, but has been called by a number of other names implying that it is simulated diamond. It is said to be much closer to diamond in appearance and hardness than any of the other substitutes.

A good way to test a cut diamond is to try its reflective qualities. Diamonds are cut to take advantage of their total reflection, which increases the fire. When looking directly into the diamond, through the upper or table facet, no part of any object behind may be seen. However, this test should be performed on absolutely clean stones, as dirt or grease on the side facets destroys the total reflection. Another method of distinguishing diamond from other stones that are crystalline is to examine it for its refraction. Because diamond shows high single refraction, the back facets appear very close, and show as clear, clean lines, not double or fuzzy as they would be in doubly refractive stones, such as zircon or quartz.

One of the best tests that can be performed with the unaided eye is the check for fire. If the stone shows a great deal of flash, it is very likely diamond; the only stone that compares with it in fire is the synthetic stone Titania, a man-made variety of the mineral titanite (sphene), which has a higher refractive index than diamond, and exhibits slightly more color flash. However, it is doubly refractive and may be identified by its refraction.

Should there still be doubt as to the identity of the stone, the best check is a microscopic one. Diamond, being crystalline and singly refractive, shows the optical characters of isotropic substances — one refractive index, no polarization of light, and so on. Glass, being noncrystalline, will not show crystallinity, and most other stones, being doubly refractive, will polarize light. Most cut stones of doubtful identity can be recognized easily by a competent jeweler or gemologist, who can also probably estimate their value.

Besides imitation diamonds, there are a few other tricks of the unscrupulous trade that buyers, if not prospectors, would do well to beware. One of these is the composite stone, comprised of two or more parts, of which one or both may be diamond. The most common among diamond composites is the doublet, of which there are two

GLOSSARY OF DIAMOND NAMES

Alaska diamond – quartz
Alençon diamond – quartz from Alençon, France
Alpine diamond – pyrite
Arkansas diamond – quartz; also true diamond from Arkansas mines
Artificial matura diamond – zircon
Australian diamond – flint glass

Baffa diamond – quartz
Bahias – diamonds from Bahia, Brazil
Black diamond – hematite
Blue-white – high-grade diamond
Bohemian diamond – quartz
Brazilian diamond – quartz or zircon; also true diamond from Brazil
Briancon diamond – quartz from southeastern France, cut in Briancon
Brilliant – glass imitation; also true diamond
Bristol diamond – quartz from Cornwall, England
By-water – yellow-tinted diamond

Canary – yellow diamond
Cape May diamond – clear quartz from Cape May, New Jersey
Cape – diamond having a yellowish tinge
Carbonado – black diamond, not crystallized
Coalinga diamond – quartz from Coalinga, California
Cornish diamond – quartz from Cornwall, England

Dauphine diamond – quartz
Diamond – diamond

False diamond – quartz
First water – pure and colorless diamond
Fleurus diamond – quartz

Golconda diamond – diamond from India

Herkimer diamond – quartz from Herkimer County, New York
Horatio diamond – diamond from Arkansas

GLOSSARY OF DIAMOND NAMES

Irish diamond – quartz from Ireland
Isle of Wight diamond – quartz
Kentucky diamond – quartz

Lake George diamond – quartz from Herkimer County, New York

Marmorosch diamond – quartz from Marmoros Comitat, Hungary
Matera diamond – dyed calcite
Matura diamond – zircon
Mora diamond – quartz

Nevada diamond – decolorized obsidian

Occidental diamond – quartz

Paphos diamond – quartz
Paste – artificial gem
Pecos diamond – quartz from Pecos River, Texas
Pennsylvania diamond – pyrite
Pseudo diamond – quartz

Quebec diamond – quartz

Ripe diamond – true diamond

Schaumburg diamond – quartz
Simulated diamond – paste
Slave's diamond – colorless topaz
Sulfur diamond – pyrite

Tasmanian diamond – topaz
Trenton diamond – quartz from Herkimer County, New York

Unripe diamond – quartz

Vallum diamond – quartz from Tanjore District, Madras, India

YAG – yttrium aluminum garnet

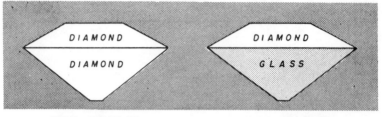

| TRUE DOUBLET | FALSE DOUBLET |

types - the false doublet and the true doublet. The true doublet consists of two small diamonds, one cut with a flat bottom and a table top, the other with a cutlet bottom and a flat top. The two are cemented together to make a stone as large as the sum of the two. The false doublet is composed of two stones, only one of which—the upper half—is diamond. Both the false and the true doublets may be identified by observing them carefully to detect the line of join. If the line cannot be readily determined by casual inspection, the stone may be immersed in an oil, preferably one of a fairly high refractive index. The line of join will then be clear (in fact, in some liquids, the cement that is commonly used will dissolve) and, if the doublet is a false one, the glass or paste that forms the lower half will not be difficult to distinguish from the true diamond of the upper half.

Obviously, two small stones (a true doublet) are not worth the price of one large stone that weighs the same, and a diamond that is half a diamond (a false doublet) is worth much less than half the worth of a diamond twice its size.

In 1955, synthetic diamonds, similar in all respects to true ones except in the manner of their origin, were made by the General Electric Company in Schenectady, New York.

Actually, reports of small diamonds having been made in the laboratory were not new; since the early nineteenth century, small stones were said to have been made using very high temperatures, but no commercial production ever resulted from any of the processes.

The most persistent claimant was J. B. Hannay, who in 1880 experimented with a mixture of hydrocarbons, bone oil, and lithium heated to a red heat in sealed iron tubes. Scientific circles were divided as to the validity of his experiment: his friends insisted he had made diamonds; official scientific societies declared he had not. In 1902 the Encyclopaedia Britannica called his diamonds "silicon carbide". Hannay protested. Years later, the diamonds he claimed to have made were taken from their repository in the British Museum for reinvestigation. They were found to be truly diamonds – but still the rumor persists that Hannay produced them by legerdemain rather than by chemical synthesis.

In 1894, fourteen years after Hannay's experiments, the French scientist Ferdinand Frederick Henri Moissan reported that he had made diamonds. His invention of the electric arc furnace shortly before, coupled with the discovery of diamonds in the meteoritic iron of Meteor Crater, Arizona (then called Canyon Diablo), spurred him to consider the synthesis of diamond. In an attempt to reproduce the conditions nature provided when the diamonds crystallized from the meteorite, he dissolved carbon in molten iron in his furnace, then cooled the mass quickly by plunging it into water or molten lead.

When he dissolved the iron in hydrochloric acid, a microscopic residue remained. He thought it was diamond, but there was then no way of testing such small stones accurately enough to determine whether they were or were not diamond. Later, his process was repeated and elaborated by Sir Charles Parsons, who reluctantly concluded that neither he nor Moissan – nor, for that matter, anyone else – had made a synthetic diamond. Unfortunately, none of the minute crystals from either man's experiments were preserved.

In 1912, Max von Laue discovered x-ray diffraction – a system of photographing powdered substances by x-ray. The resulting picture consists of a series of lines that are distinctive for each element. In this way, all of the elements in a substance can be determined. It was this method that allowed the exact determination of Hannay's diamonds. How annoyed Hannay must have been if he had produced the diamonds in his laboratory and no one had believed him; how much more annoyed he must have been if he had "salted" the experiment with real diamonds and no one had recognized them!

The General Electric Company success indicates clearly that high temperatures and high pressures are essential. The company began experimenting with the production of synthetic diamonds as early as 1941, when it, jointly with Carborundum and Norton Companies, supported the research of the Harvard physicist, Percy W. Bridgman. Dr. Bridgman developed an apparatus that could exert pressures as great as a million and a half pounds per square inch, together with temperatures as high as 3000° C. for a few seconds. Although he did not succeed in producing diamonds, his experiments clearly pointed the way.

The U.S. Signal Corps, too, experimented with the production of synthetic diamonds. Both Bridgman and the Corps used a metallic flux - in both cases, nickel. The Signal Corps apparatus consisted of a chamber only half an inch in diameter, in which a layer of graphite—a mineral form of carbon long in common commercial use as "lead" in pencils—was sandwiched between layers of nickel surrounded by pyrophyllite. The diamonds formed on the contact between nickel and graphite. The Corps could only attain a maximum temperature of $1560°$ C. and a pressure of 1,300,000 pounds per square inch, but diamonds as large as half a millimeter in diameter formed within three minutes. The color ranged from green to yellow, depending upon the temperature.

General Electric's giant two-story press is enormous compared to the small one the Corps worked with. It is capable of sustaining continuous pressure as great as a million and a half pounds per square inch, and a temperature as high as $2,700°$ C. The reaction that produces diamonds takes place in a doughnut-shaped chamber, in which some form of carbon is sandwiched between nickel, in a pyrophyllite gasket, as in the Corps' experiments. A great many forms of carbon were used—newspaper reports indicated that even peanut butter was tried—but graphite again proved to be the best choice.

General Electric, too, found that the diamonds appeared only at the junction of the nickel and graphite, but the long period of time in which they could maintain the high temperature and pressure allowed diamonds as large as a sixteenth of an inch to crystallize.

General Electric's interest is not principally in gem quality stones, but in an assured supply of industrial diamonds. John D. Kennedy, an engineer from General Electric's Metallurgical Products Development branch, stated in a paper presented to the American Institute of Mining and Metallurgical Engineers that there was now no reason for the United States to be concerned about its supply of industrial diamonds. If needed, Mr. Kennedy said, the company could meet the entire United States demand for abrasive diamonds.

In September, 1962, General Electric announced another breakthrough in diamond manufacture: diamonds could now be made without using the nickel catalyst. Carbon could be induced to change directly from graphite into diamond. This new advance, coupled with the production of larger crystals and crystals designed for special uses,

Cherokee Assay Office, Butte County

has made industrial diamonds more useful and available than ever before.

While they were casting about for methods and machinery to produce synthetic diamonds for commerce, research workers at GE did not neglect to test both Hannay's and Moissan's old techniques. Hannay's procedure yielded only amorphous carbon; a repetition of Moissan's experiments, too, gave only graphite.

But success breeds success. Once GE had broken the ice, other companies in the United States have found that they, too, can manufacture synthetic diamonds. So can laboratories in Sweden, South Africa, Ireland, and Japan. The Irish and South African facilities are owned by the De Beers Syndicate, who own the South African diamond fields. They have been marketing synthetic diamonds, more or less in competition with themselves, since 1962. Although Russia claims to have produced stones in the laboratory, none of their experimental results have been published.

Although synthetic diamonds are produced at present only for the industrial market, worried diamond buyers may be glad to know that it is easily possible to tell synthetic stones from natural ones by laboratory tests. All diamonds, natural and man made, carry hallmarks that betray their source. These are tiny impurities, or "inclusions" that are not the same in the two types of stones. For example, nitrogen, an important impurity in diamond, is found as little platelets in natural stones, but is dispersed throughout the molecular structure of synthetic ones. Where the nitrogen comes from to enter the diamond crystal is a mystery.

The industrial uses (that is, the non-gem uses) of diamond are many and varied. So great is the demand for industrial stones that the market price for the lowest quality, or bort, is about $7,000 per pound; for higher grade cutting stones (still not good enough to qualify as gems), the price is as high as a million dollars per pound. In terms of carats, the price of natural industrial diamonds ranges from $2.85 for ungraded fines; synthetic diamonds, which entered the market at a price of $5.10 per carat, are now priced almost like natural ones.

WHERE TO LOOK FOR DIAMONDS

One of the best places to look for the diamond—just as for any other mineral—is where it has already been found. The discovery of a mineral is a hopeful sign that conditions may have been right for its accumulation in paying quantity in that place. This axiom, known to scientists as the concept of "metallogenic provinces" or "mineral provinces", is so obvious that most persons know it without thinking about it. It is the basic principle behind mining rushes of all kinds: one handful of gold, or a rise in the pulse of a geiger counter, is a siren call to prospectors the world over.

Fortunately for the mineral collector or diamond prospector, quite a few diamonds have been found in California. They were not found in the rock in which they were originally formed, but instead in the beds of streams; either in the beds of streams that now drain the mountain reaches of the State, or in the beds of the ancestral streams that thousands of years ago flowed down the mountain fronts by different routes. Almost all of them were found in the course of mining for gold in these old and new stream deposits; how many others were discarded, unrecognized, is not known.

The oldest diamond mines in the world are in India, where the gem is recovered from gravel deposits that in many ways resemble the gravel deposits of California. The Indian diggings, so ancient that the date of their discovery has passed into the realm of fable, have provided diamonds for untold generations; indeed, until the discovery of the Brazilian deposits in 1725, the Indian deposits (and some in Borneo known prior to the sixteenth century) were the only sources of diamonds for the trade of the civilized world.

The Indian diggings lie near the ruined city of Golconda, a few miles from modern Hyderabad. All of the mines are placer workings of a sort; that is, the diamonds are recovered by washing gravel deposited in the beds of ancient and modern rivers. Though all of the diamonds found so far have been washed down from some primeval source, some of them are found in beds of gravel so cemented that more heroic methods than simple digging must be used to break the material. A common, though primitive, expedient was to set a brush fire, heat the face of the rock, and dash it with cold water, causing it to split.

California and Indian diamonds are alike in three ways. First, the environment in which they are found is similar. In both places, the diamonds have been recovered from modern stream gravel, and from stream gravel deposited in rivers that flowed through the country in past ages. It is possible to trace some of the material in modern Indian rivers to its source in the older, higher stream beds; the rocks in the older stream beds, in turn, can be traced to a consolidated gravel. The source of the consolidated gravel — now conglomerate — is not known, but the conglomerate itself is Precambrian in age, and therefore among the world's oldest rocks. None of the California diamonds have been found in rocks as old as these.

A second point of resemblance is the shape of the diamonds themselves. Both the Indian and California stones are commonly octahedral (eight-sided) in shape; not so the Brazilian stones, which are commonly dodecahedral, or twelve-sided.

The third similarity between California and Indian diamonds is shared by the Brazilian stones as well: the source of all three is a mystery. In India, the rocks that were the source of the old conglomerate

Diamond washing near Golconda, 1859

A Brazilian diamond convoy, 1869

beds were probably worn down many millions of years ago and either washed into the sea or hidden beyond hope of discovery. In Brazil, also, the mother lode has not been found; though some who have studied the mines argue that a much-altered soft rock in the area is the original diamond host, this has not been proved. In Brazil, too, the new material in the stream beds and the debris from older rivers enclose diamonds. In Brazil, as in India, the rocks composing the gravels can be traced to sedimentary beds of Precambrian age, but they, too, are from an unknown source.

The ancestral line of California diamonds is not so old. They have been found in the present-day rivers, mixed with pebbles that came from the rocks that comprise the mountains today, and in the beds of former rivers, reworked, in places, by the newer streams. These older beds, also, are derived from rocks similar to those in the hills today, indicating that the source rock may still exist. Nowhere in California is there any indication that the diamonds are older than a hundred million years, or roughly a tenth the age of the Brazilian and Indian stones.

Brazilian diamonds, like the few diamonds from California, were found in placer deposits during the search for gold. The batea, a wide, shallow wooden vessel exported from South America during the California gold rush, was used in Brazil for diamond and gold mining for more than a century before the California rush.

Nineteenth century African diamond workings

CALIFORNIA DIAMONDS IN PLACER

Though all of the diamonds found in California so far are small, and no discoveries have been made that portend a vast, rich diamond field, there is no reason why an enterprising mineral collector should not find a stone for his collection, provided he is sufficiently patient and lucky. It is, of course, not beyond reason that a large field does exist; the chief argument against that possibility is that no such field has yet been found.

During the 1880s, quite a bit of interest in diamond hunting was stirred up in California, probably a reflection of the fevered rush of the decade past to the newly opened diamond fields in South Africa, where fortunes of lucky prospectors were made by a single stone. The pattern of this rush was like all mining rushes; millions for a few, very little for most.

The stay-at-homes in California eagerly took counsel with the experts mining engineers, mineralogists, anyone just home from Africa — and the pros and cons of diamond prospecting were argued in the newspapers and scientific journals of the day.

"I would not recommend any one to institute a special hunt for diamonds," wrote W. A. Goodyear, a member of the staff of the California Geological Survey, "since at best they are not remarkably plenty. But it does no harm and takes no time to keep one eye upon the contents of the pan while engaged in cleaning up sluices, batteries, etc., in working the gravel, and though it may not pay to hunt for diamonds, yet it always pays to pick them up when you do happen to see them."

Mr. Goodyear's statement, which may well be the most conservative advice ever given a miner, was published in 1872, when the potentialities of the African fields had barely been glimpsed.

In another ten years, the Geological Survey had been replaced by the State Mining Bureau, and the new (and first) State Mineralogist, Henry G. Hanks, was in charge. He was considerably more optimistic concerning the future of California diamond mining, arguing that a diamond field in the State was a distinct possibility — or, at the worst, that diamonds were almost certain to be an important by-product of gold mining, particularly hydraulic mining, wherein tremendous streams of water were thrown against the gold-bearing gravel banks. Hanks deplored the unfortunate techniques of this system of mining, which washed everything but the gold – and some of that– toward the sea.

"The resident manager [of the Cherokee mine,"] wrote Mr. Hanks in 1882, "admitted that the mechanical force of the stream of water used washed away platinum and associated minerals which do not amalgamate with the quicksilver used to arrest the gold, entailing a loss for which there is now no known remedy. I have alluded elsewhere to the imperfect method of hydraulic mining, and do not hesitate to express the opinion that when these defects are remedied both diamonds and platinum will become important mineral products of the State."

But hydraulic mining was never perfected sufficiently to make diamonds a commercial product in California. A scant eleven years after Mr. Hanks wrote of the possibility of recovering a considerable number of diamonds from hydraulic mines, the Caminetti Act, passed in the

How hydraulic mining is done. Scene in the Cherokee pit, Butte County, California, where many diamonds were discovered. From an old print.

Congress of the United States, emasculated most of the hydraulic mines by preventing the dumping of debris in navigable rivers.

Nevertheless, Mr. Hanks did not lose heart. "It has long been my opinion," he said in an address before the San Francisco Microscopical Society, "that if hydraulic mining had been allowed to continue, a system of concentration would have been adopted, resulting in a greater production of gold and platinum, and in the finding of more diamonds.

"It is not yet unlikely that they may be found in California more plentifully than before."

Hanks, a local man, was not the only expert to investigate the possibility that California would be another Transvaal. Soon those who had rushed to Africa were returning, and others who had worked in Africa passed through, and all gave their opinions. One Mr. Atkins, a "diamond expert from South Africa", was reported by the San Francisco Call in 1888 to have "examined the diamond-bearing placers at Cherokee and Volcano."

Mr. Atkins concluded that the gravel fields in which the diamonds were found were not their original bed. Inasmuch as this was the same view held by the gold miners who had worked the deposits for thirty years, his contribution startled no one. He was not, however, enthusiastic about California diamond possibilities.

"Mr. Atkins," the Call reported, "did not think California a promising field for the diamond prospectors, and left for the Puget Sound region, since when nothing has been heard from him."

At least one person was not discouraged by the pessimism of the retreating Atkins. Henry Videl, mining superintendent of Amador, gave a long interview to the San Francisco Examiner the following year, in which he was quoted as commenting enthusiastically, "Just take a look at this big diamond," and concluding with "I predict that diamonds [will be found] in sufficient quantities to handsomely pay...and that, within a year, diamond mining will be a business in Amador and Butte Counties."

Mr. Videl's predictions have not been vindicated. Diamond mining is not, and has not been an economic industry anywhere in California. All of the diamonds found have been small, and in no place has a sizeable pocket or concentration of stones yet been discovered. Nonetheless, diamonds have been picked up in at least fifteen counties, from placer deposits that indisputably had their source within the borders of the State or very close by. It is by no means impossible that a large alluvial field, similar to those in Brazil, has been overlooked in California.

All but a very few of the California stones have been found in the Sierra Nevada, during the course of gold mining. The first was probably found about 1849, though the earliest date recorded is 1853, when a diamond was recognized in the sluice of the Cherokee Flat hydraulic mine in Butte County. From this mine in its heyday millions of yards of gravel were moved; it produced some thirteen million dollars (as of 1911) worth of gold, as well as more than three hundred diamonds. The largest stone recorded from Cherokee weighed about two and one-quarter carats, though local rumor tells of a diamond as large as six carats.

The last diamond of any size reported from within the bounds of the State was a 2.66 carat stone found in 1934 near Plymouth, in Amador County. However, microscopic diamonds have been seen in sands of the ocean beaches of Monterey and San Mateo Counties.

None of the diamonds found so far has come unquestionably from the original source rock. All of them, so far as can be proved, have been found in ancient or modern river channels or beach sands. In

Diamond found near Plymouth, Amador County. Length, 8.5 mm.; width, 6.1 mm.; thickness, 5.7 mm.; weight, half a gram, or about 2.5 carats.

the Sierra Nevada, the diamonds are associated closely with placer gold deposits; they trace their history to the same period of erosion that scoured the placer gold from its parent rock, and found their resting place in the same fossil stream channels.

The location of modern rivers is to be found on any detailed map; the ancient rivers, because they are mostly buried, are not so well known. A few have been mapped, though their courses are imperfectly traced, and whole river beds, as well as countless tributaries, may be undiscovered.

Records show that nine Sierran counties have yielded diamonds. Of the nine, Amador, Butte, and El Dorado have been the most prolific. The other six—Nevada, Placer, Plumas, Stanislaus, Tulare, and Tuolumne—have produced only one or, at most, a few minute diamonds each.

AMADOR COUNTY

Five places in Amador County have provided small diamonds. At three of them, the diamonds were definitely in old river channels - probably the Tertiary Mokelumne River or a tributary. The other two sources may have been either modern rivers or buried channels; the reports which have been preserved do not specify which.

At Volcano, the best known Amador County locality, the stones were recovered from an old channel about 40 feet under a volcanic formation described by J. D. Whitney, the second State Geologist, as "ashes and pumice cemented by water." More than sixty diamonds were found at Volcano, in addition to splinters and diamond dust seen in mill tailings. The exact location of the find was Jackass Gulch, almost within the present town of Volcano. The gulch is now entered by the road passing east of the Armory, opposite the old brewery.

Twenty diamonds were found about 1865 by Chris Wisner from this locality, all in the space of about three months. One diamond was said to have been sold for $33.

In 1882, A. Schmitz found a diamond "at Volcano." It weighed about a carat and a half, was about three-tenths of an inch long, in the shape of an octahedron. It was clear and colorless, but somewhat flawed.

At Fiddletown (at various times known as Oleta), the diamonds came from Loafer Hill, and, like those from Volcano, were found in gravel underlying ash. Some diamonds were found here as early as 1855; the largest recorded was approximately 1.33 carats.

Indian Gulch, east of Amador City, is also cited as a diamond locality, though few details are published. G. F. Kunz, writing in 1905,

Topographic map of the Volcano area, where diamonds were found.

stated that the stones – he knew of five – were from a gray "cement gravel". The exact location of the discovery is not given, but Indian Gulch carries a small, intermittent stream that flows west for about two miles, joins the intermittent streams that drain Kanaka and Whiskey Gulches to the south, and enters Amador Creek. The Sutter Creek fifteen-minute topographic quadrangle published in 1944 (scale about one inch to the mile) shows this gulch. The map may be purchased from the U.S. Geological Survey, Denver Federal Center, Denver, Colorado.

A pale straw-colored diamond weighing about a carat was found by George Evans on the surface of the gravel at Rancheria – some four miles northwest of Volcano – in July 1883. Here an ancient river channel covered by consolidated volcanic ash is directly in front of the site of the old Rancheria store, the "Stone Jug". Its exact location is SW¼NW¼ sec. 18, T. 7 N., R. 12 E., M.D. The property is privately owned.

Little is known about the fifth Amador County locality, save that it is near Plymouth. The only diamond reported from here was found in 1934 by Robert F. Echols of Plymouth, weighed 2.57 carats, and was a colorless, transparent crystal.

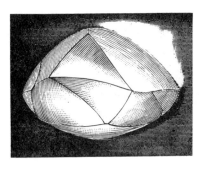

Amador County diamond, magnified about seven times. The stone has not been cut; the faces shown are all natural. Its weight was 255 milligrams; its length three-tenths of an inch. Pale and straw colored, this stone was nearly flawless. The diamond was found by George Evans in July, 1883, on the surface of the ground at the now deserted mining camp of Rancheria near Volcano.

Upper Rancheria in the 1950s

BUTTE COUNTY

The Oroville area, in Butte County, was and is California's most famous diamond locality, including particularly Cherokee Flat, location of the immense Cherokee hydraulic mine developed by the Spring Valley Mining Company. From this mine, situated near the North Fork of the Feather River about eight miles north of Oroville, more than three hundred diamonds have been recovered, according to official estimates, which are based on skimpy and scattered records, and, in part, hearsay. Some of the diamonds were recovered by miners working in the mine, and became the property of the Spring Valley Mining Company; others were kept by the miners, probably with the Company's permission; still others were gathered by "fossickers". An attempt was made to mine the pit for diamonds under the auspices of the U.S. Diamond Mining Company. For much of the life of the Company, access was freely given to all who wished to prospect. Under these circumstances, any records of the diamond production of the district can only represent a small protion of the true production.

The first diamond taken from the Cherokee pit was said to have been found in 1852 or 1853; since these are the same dates given for the first use of hydraulic equipment in California, that is very early, indeed. The largest stone recorded, found in 1868 by John Moore, weighed six carats; stones of several shades, including pure white, rose, and yellow, have been seen. Two diamonds found by N. A. Harris, superintendent of the mine at Cherokee, were mounted in rings. One is a beautiful natural crystal, the other a cut stone of fine quality. Both are on display in the mineral exhibit of the California Division of Mines and Geology in San Francisco, together with a rough diamond from Volcano.

A diamond was reported from the Cherokee pit in 1930; no doubt a number of others has been found there and not reported in any way that would allow them to be officially recorded.

Oliver E. Bowen, retired mining geologist of the California Division of Mines and Geology, who in 1958 made a study of the Cherokee hydraulic pit with a view to charting its mineral potential—particularly the resources of sand, gravel, and clay—found several small diamonds.

South of Cherokee and two miles north of Oroville is Thompson Flat, another Butte County diamond locality. Like the diamonds from Cherokee, those from Thompson Flat were found in placer workings in

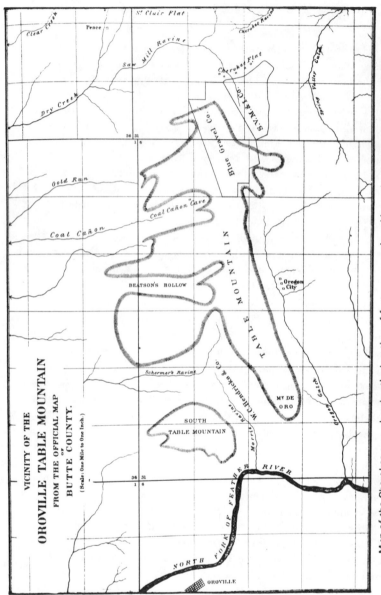

Map of the Cherokee area, showing the location of features mentioned by early diamond hunters in California.

an old Tertiary channel. Cherokee mine is at the north end of a volcanic flow called, in company with many other flat-topped volcanic flows, Table Mountain. Thompson Flat is at the south end of this flow, south of a breach cut by a modern river. The south part of the flow, separated by the breach from the main portion, is called, imaginatively, South Table Mountain. The Tertiary Cherokee channel deposits, from which both Cherokee and Thompson Flat obtained their gold and diamonds, is covered and preserved by the Table Mountain lava flow. Although the Cherokee workings, the mines near Thompson Flat, and drift and other hydraulic mines have moved millions of yards of gravel, a great deal still remains beneath the hard cover of Table Mountain.

The source of the channel itself is not known. Its relation to the old drainage that has been traced some miles to the east is still a mystery, though the pay streaks within the part of the channel mined were more than a thousand feet wide and have been worked for a mile and a half in length.

Besides those taken from the old channels, a few diamonds have been panned from modern rivers. In 1895, Dwight Whiting reported finding five small diamonds near Oroville on the Feather River, and more about four miles from the head of a creek that his statement does not name.

A rather famous California diamond is the one taken from a placer mine a mile and a half northwest of Yankee Hill in Butte County, in the course of cleaning up the sluice. It was purchased by M. H. Wells, who presented it to John Bidwell, one of California's best-remembered pre-gold-rush settlers. Mr. Bidwell had it cut in Boston into a one and one-half carat stone for his wife, who wore it in a ring for many years.

EL DORADO COUNTY

The records of diamonds found in El Dorado County are more nearly complete, and probably more accurate, than for any other Sierran county. Though the whole of El Dorado County did not produce as many diamonds as did the Cherokee pit, the history of the stones is better known — mostly because of the efforts of one man, Judge William Pitt Carpender. Judge Carpender, an old-time miner and El Dorado County resident, came to Smiths Flat in 1854 from Akron, Ohio, via the Nicaragua route, and was justice of the peace at Placerville for

FINDER	DATE	LOCALITY
John Bradshaw	1859	Buchanan mine, Smiths Flat
John Lyford	1865	Smiths Flat
A. Brooks	1866	Spanish Ravine
Ward (Wood?) Bros.	1867	Near White Rock Cañon
Thos. Ward & Co.	1868	Live Oak mine, Reservoir Hill
Thomas Potts Sr.	1868	Near White Rock Cañon
J. Jeffry (Jeffery)		Webber Hill
Mrs. Sam Henderson	1868	Wisconsin Flat mine
Cruson & Olmstead	1868	Wisconsin Flat mine (Unity mine)
Henry Olmstead	1869	Cruson tunnel, Dirty Flat
Henry Ashcroft	1869(?)	Smiths Flat region
Charles Reed	1870	McConnell & Reed mine south side Webber Hill and east side Texas Hill
Nathaniel O. Ames		Mine on Webber Hill
	1874?	Smiths Flat
	1874?	Smiths Flat
	1870-90	Smiths Flat region
Chas. W. Schafer		Tockey mine, Texas Hill
Fred Bendfeldt Sr.	1878	Smiths Flat
Ed Randall	1879	Wisconsin Flat mine
Jacob Lyon	Pre-1882	Lyon mine (?)

WT.*	COLOR	REMARKS
	White	Small
0.97	White	Stolen by a woman and set rough in a ring
0.65	White	Flawed
		Three small stones, largest valued at $50 in S.F.
	2 white 1 yellow	Three stones, 2 white of medium size, 1 set in ring once in the possession of a Mr. Ashcroft of Oakland, who had it cut in England
0.65	Light yellow	Sold to W. A. Goodyear when he visited mines at Smiths Flat in 1871, for $15; small, flawed
0.97	Yellow	
	White	Medium size
		Four stones
1.82		Pure, nearly round, white coating on surface; max. diam. 9/32-in.; found during sluice clean-up; sold for $280 to Mr. Tucker in S. F.
		Reported by F. F. Barss, Placerville jeweler; may be stone found by T. Ward & Co.
	Canary yellow	Size of small white bean; Mrs. Caleb Reed of Placerville had it set in a ring
1.30		Set in ring and worn by Shelly Inch, postmaster, Placerville, for many years; later owned by L. P. Inch, city manager of a San Francisco fire insurance company
0.10		Purchased by F. F. Barss, jeweler of Placerville, from a Chinese man
0.10		Good stone purchased by Barss from miner Barss reported he set 5 diamonds in breastpins and 2 in rings, all good stones, for different people; one had piece of "original" blue matrix attached to it
0.18		Sold to John Cook
0.45	Canary	Sold to W. F. Alma of Boston
0.13	White	
	Light straw	About size of medium-sized pea; also several fragments from tailing of gravel mill at mine

47

FINDER	DATE	LOCALITY
F. Bendfeldt	Pre-1882	
W. P. Carpender	Pre-1894	Carpender's section of old channel, near Placerville
Fred Bendfeldt, Jr.	1894	Smiths Flat
Bert Carpender	1896	Smiths Flat
Thomas Murdoch	1896	Smiths Flat
Snow Bros.	1897	Near Newton (Newtown?)
Snow Bros.	1897	Near Fairplay
Bert Carpender	1899	Stanley mine, Smiths Flat
Fred Bosworth	1900	Cedar Ravine, Placerville
J. Allen	1901	Cedar Ravine, Placerville
	1906-09	Neocene river channel between Placerville and Smiths Flat
	1906-09	Neocene river channel between Placerville and Smiths Flat
Bert Carpender	1912	Carpender mine
Frank Jones	1914(?)	Jones' gravel mine in Chile Ravine

*Weight in metric carats

thirty-two years. He kept careful track of all the diamonds that came to his attention, and made a special effort to obtain the correct facts about each. His life (he died in February, 1916 at the age of eighty-five) spanned the time of most of the diamond discoveries.

Judge Carpender's list of diamonds found in the Placerville region includes stones from Live Oak mine on Reservoir Hill, Smiths Flat,

WT.*	COLOR	REMARKS
	Yellow	Small, 2 grains; passed through gravel mill
	Greenish (larger) Yellowish (smaller)	Two stones, each nearly a quarter of an inch in diameter
0.96	White	Sold to W. F. Alma
1.92	White	Three stones sold to W. F. Alma
0.26	White	
1.67	Canary	
1.07	Yellow	Sold to W. F. Alma
1.54	White	
0.97	Canary	In possession of Geo. Richardson [in 1882]
0.65	White	In possession of W. P. Stanley [in 1882]
1.46	White	Up to $80 offered for the rough stone
0.42	White	Sold to W. F. Alma
0.10 to 1.00		N. H. Burger, Placerville jeweler, set 4 stones he had cut in New York in rings for different people
0.36	Blue	Fine stone set in ring by N. H. Burger, Placerville jeweler
0.97	White	
0.50	White	Good stone set in ring for Jones by Burger

Spanish Ravine, White Rock Ravine, Webber Hill, Wisconsin Flat mine, Texas Hill, Newtown, Fairplay, and Prospect Flat. Judge Carpender provided information about diamonds as early as 1882, when a query directed by Mr. Hanks, the State Mineralogist, to the postmaster at Placerville (for want of a more knowledgeable person) was forwarded to Mr. Carpender, who answered it. His last, most comprehensive list, given with additions herein, was published in 1916.

NEVADA COUNTY

At French Corral, Nevada County, two diamonds have been found, according to reports. One weighed 1.33 carats, the other somewhat more. They were found in buried gravel, both before 1900.

PLACER COUNTY

One diamond, weighing a carat and a half, was found at Forest Hill, in Placer County. It came from a "great depth" in a tunnel run into the gold-bearing gravel. This locality is here listed as in Placer County, assuming that it was found at Forest Hill, though early reports (and recent ones as well) list it as in El Dorado.

PLUMAS COUNTY

Diamonds ranging in size from microscopic to about two carats have been found at four places in Plumas County. At two of the localities, Gopher Hill (sec. 7, T. 24 N., R. 9 E., M.D.) and Spanish Creek (sec. 10, T. 24 N., R. 8 E., M.D.), diamonds were found in black sands rich in heavy minerals.

Diamonds from the other two places, Sawpit Flat (section 31, T. 23 N., R. 10 E. and section 6, T. 22 N., R. 10 E.), shown on the Onion Valley seven-and-a-half-minute topographic quadrangle map, and Nelson Point (on the Feather River), were found in Tertiary river channels.

Two stones are known to have come from Sawpit Flat; the second of these was found by Ed. Bryan, a miner, who stated that it was "very similar to a diamond found at the locality several years ago and known to be authentic." In his letter to the Sacramento Union published August 17, 1913, Mr. Bryan admitted that there was some doubt that his find was a true diamond (though it probably was) because the stone was "lost through misplaced confidence" before he was positive of the identification.

STANISLAUS COUNTY

According to the *San Joaquin Republican* of 1860, "...a party of miners were working a claim with sluice and hydraulic pipe and hose, at a point called Buena Vista, nearly opposite Knight's Ferry. One night about dark, the pipeman saw an object which he had washed out of the bank, lie glittering in the pile of dirt and stones, that was about to be passed through the sluice. The gleams from it lit up all the space in the vicinity, and caused much astonishment to the hardy workmen. The pipeman picked it up and moved along to show it to one of his comrades, but accidentally dropped it into the sluice, and it was borne down by the torrent of water into the mass of stones and dirt known as 'tailings'. A company of Spiritualists at Knight's Ferry are trying to discover the present locality of the jewel, which is represented to be larger than the Koh-i-noor."

TULARE COUNTY

One small diamond was found on the bank of Alpine Creek by L. W. Hawkins about 1899.

TUOLUMNE COUNTY

The *California Mining Journal* in its second issue, dated May, 1856, gave the following information regarding diamonds from Tuolumne County:

"Discovery of Diamonds.— A Mr. Helt has exhibited to the editor of the *Sonora Herald* two very beautiful, but small specimens of diamond which were found in the mining claim of Messrs. Helt and Pierce, on Shaw's Flat, near the Columbia road. The diamonds have been pronounced to be the *simon pure* article by Dr. Snell, a learned geologist and chemist. They were found with the gold after panning out."

OTHER LOCALITIES

Not all California diamonds have been found in the Sierra Nevada. Some have come from the ocean beaches from Monterey into San Mateo County, though they may be separated from the sand of which they are a part and identified only by the aid of a powerful microscope. In 1916 a rumor was current that diamonds had been found in Imperial County along the San Diego border, but no substantiation has ever been published.

Diamonds have been found in the Klamath Mountains, some in placer gravels at Hamburg Bar in Siskiyou County (in the extreme northeast corner of T. 45 N., R. 11 E., M.D., on the Klamath River), but most of them from the drainage area of the Smith and Trinity Rivers, in Del Norte, Humboldt, and Trinity Counties. All so far reported except one – have been very small. That one stone, supposedly a diamond from Trinity County, was lost, but was said to be about half an inch in size. According to the *Mining and Scientific Press* of March, 1871, the *Trinity Journal* of February 25, 1871 told of its finding in these words:

"Several years ago, Mr. I. Woodbury, while mining the red flat above Garden Gulch, found a singular looking stone in his bedrock ditch and picked it up. As it lay in the ditch it appeared to be a piece of metal, but upon closer inspection it showed to be a stone having a glazed metallic coating. The crust was broken off on one side apparently by a blow from a pick, revealing the grain of the stone. Mr. Woodbury thought it was a queer looking pebble and so thinking laid it up on the side of the ditch and went about his work.

"Passing on a few feet, he had occasion to turn around to give directions to some person behind him, when his attention was arrested by the strange results produced by the sunbeams falling on the odd seeming pebble. The fractured side happened to be up and reflected the sun's rays in a brilliant flame mainly of a bluish tint, but showing the various tints of the rainbow and blazing up in size and shape much like a large dining glass. Never having seen the like before, Mr. Woodbury thought to keep it as a curiosity and told his brother to put it away. Having read an article in the *Mining and Scientific Press* in relation to these precious stones, Mr. Woodbury became satisfied that it was a diamond that so much enlisted his curiosity. After making diligent search and inquiry he has been unable to find it. The mislaid diamond was half an inch or more in diameter, and being doubtless of the first water was of great value, perhaps running well up into thousands.

"Moral—Miners don't be careless with odd looking pebbles or pieces of metal. Fortune may come knocking at your door and be entertained unawares or worse yet you may slam the door in her face."

CALIFORNIA DIAMONDS IN LODE

Where any of the diamonds found so far in California came from originally is still a mystery. It is quite logical and probable that all of them came from rocks that are or were within the borders of the State; whether these rocks have been completely removed by the processes of erosion, whether they have been covered by the products of erosion, or whether they are simply undiscovered, has been the source of much speculation.

At a few places in the world, diamonds are found in what have long been considered to be the necks of old volcanoes. The richest of the world's diamond fields are the "diamond pipes" found over a large area in South Africa, Southwest Africa, Rhodesia, Tanganyika, (Tanzania), and southeastern Congo. Numerous books and articles have been written about these diamond fields, particularly about the origin of the rocks that contain the diamonds, but as yet no one has found a wholly satisfactory explanation as to why the stones are there.

The diamonds are found in a peculiar rock known as "kimberlite". This is the core of the pipe. It is a very basic igneous rock — that is, a dark rock containing a very little silica but a great deal of lime, iron and magnesium, now altered considerably to serpentine. Surrounding the pipes and cut by them are horizontally bedded rocks: quartzitic sandstone, volcanic flows, and shale. Near the top of the pipes, the kimberlite is badly weathered — miners call it "yellow ground". Deeper in the pipes the color of the rock is darker, giving rise to the name "blue ground".

The blue ground, or less severely weathered material, contains fragments of carbonaceous shale torn from the rocks through which the pipe made its way. Since carbon is a relatively rare element in rocks that come from deep within the earth, some early investigators thought that the carbon making up the diamonds (diamonds are pure carbon) was derived from the shale beds. This is an easy answer, but, unfortunately, most of the clues point in another direction.

It is fairly certain on the basis of evidence so far uncovered that the diamonds were a part of the fluid rock, at the time it began its ascent up the pipe. Diamond crystals have been seen intergrown with the mineral garnet and with other heavy, dark minerals; they have been found in fresh, unweathered rock, enclosed so tightly that it is obvious that they solidified as part of the rock.

One kind of fresh rock in which they have been found is the rare type eclogite—a dark heavy rock consisting chiefly of garnet and the black mineral pyroxene. The rock is known in very few places in the world, South Africa and California claiming the best exposures.

Whatever the source of the diamonds in the kimberlite pipes, that they are in kimberlite is apparently of considerable importance. If they were added to the pipe as a geologic afterthought, picked up, perhaps, somewhere en route, the fact that the pipe is kimberlite should be of little consequence—hot, fluid material of any composition might do as well. Such is not the case. Either the diamonds have an unusual, unexplained affinity for kimberlite, or—more likely—they were an essential part of the original kimberlite. Strong evidence of the importance of kimberlite is provided by the discovery of diamonds in Arkansas in rock very similar to the African kimberlite pipes, yet thousands of miles from them.

In Nevada, a discovery of three diamonds by Kent Maher of Pershing County, indicated that diamonds in lode might possibly be found there. Mr. Maher stated, according to the Denver *Mining Record*, that his stones were obtained "when exploring a blue mud 'pipe' in Dixie Valley." The nearby area contains considerable volcanic rock, a hopeful sign, but no published information as to whether or not the blue mud pipe is kimberlite has been released.

So far, no true kimberlite has been found in California, though serpentine and ultrabasic rocks are widespread. Kimberlite discoveries have been reported, but each time the rock turned out to be different in some respect from the South African and Arkansas kimberlite.

The best organized attempt to find the mother of California diamonds was that of the U.S. Diamond Mining Company near Cherokee. The company was short lived; its activities lasted but a few years, and its production was low. It was formed following the discovery about 1906 of a "diamond pipe" judged to be similar to the diamond-bearing pipes of South Africa. Mr. M. J. Cooney, who later directed the company, made the discovery about a mile north of Oroville along the west bank of the Feather River. Here, hydraulic mining had stripped some twenty to sixty feet of cover from the surface, revealing the "blue rock"—a soft, highly serpentinized, obviously altered material. Samples of the rock were sent to the U.S. Geological Survey for comparison with the South African kimberlite; Douglas B. Sterrett, who compared them, gave this opinion:

"The specimens [from California] marked 'blue' were soft, highly serpentinized rocks whose original nature could not be determined. In a thin section under the microscope the rock was found to contain rounded crystals of some mineral, probably olivine, entirely altered to serpentine. The section contained a great deal of serpentine throughout, with some in little streaks and veinlets. There were small fragments, apparently a variety of feldspar, of some larger crystals, mostly lost in grinding. In hand specimens portions of the rock have a brecciated appearance, while other pieces appear to have a more even texture. The color is dull, ranging from greenish to bluish green to bluish black. Slickenside partings are not uncommon in various directions through the small pieces examined. Specimens of two other types of rock were 'bull's-eyes', or spherical balls with concentric layer structure, and concretions or nodules of calcium carbonate. The 'bull's-eyes' range in size from that of an egg up, and have been formed by the weathering of a fine-grained basic rock, probably of the basalt or diabase family. It has a fine porphyritic texture with a slight development of amygdules.

"According to Mr. Cooney, the 'bull's-eyes' and lime nodules were found on the surface and to a depth of 20 feet, mixed with earthy material and somewhat cemented together. This gradually gave place to soft yellow ground at 25 feet. The yellow ground held out to a depth of 40 feet, where a semisiliceous stratum, 'somewhat like the "floating reefs" encountered in the diamond chutes or pipes of South Africa,' was met. Below this came in the 'blue ground' described above. The following minerals are reported by Mr. Cooney in the Oroville serpentine or 'blue' and 'yellow' earths as similar to those minerals commonly associated with the diamonds in South Africa: Menaccanite, magnetite, olivine, garnets, spinel rubies, topaz, beryl, chrysoprase, agate and other forms of chalcedony, zircons, etc.

"The specimens sent to the Survey by Mr. Cooney as typical 'blue' earth' of the Oroville locality do not bear much resemblance to the genuine kimberlite of South Africa. Points of likeness are the extensive serpentinization in each, a general bluish-green color, and probable brecciation of the California rock compared with the evident extreme brecciation of the kimberlite. On the other hand, the general appearance of the two rocks on close inspection is very unlike. The California serpentine apparently does not contain inclusions of other types of rocks forming the walls, while the kimberlite contains these in quantity, as black shale, conglomerate, quartzite, melaphyre, etc. The numerous plates of biotite common in the true kimberlite were not observed in the California rock. The presence of feldspathic material in the California serpentine indicated a quite different type of rock from the kimberlite. The latter is regarded as a serpentinized volcanic peridotite breccia, with the serpentine probably derived from a less basic rock, possibly of the gabbro or diorite class. As far as can be learned, the presence of 'bull's-eyes' is not a prominent feature of the South African diamond mines, while the occurrence of lime concretions is not limited to the outcrop of diamond pipes alone, but is common to large areas of the country around Kimberley, where rocks other than kimberlite outcrop.

"It seems likely that the outcrop of rock near Oroville, designated 'kimberlite' by Mr. Cooney, is a portion of one of the belts of serpentinized amphibolite schists running through the country in a northwest direction...The alluvium has been washed off, exposing a portion of such a belt, which has been mistaken for a pipe formation, since it is exposed over a limited area. The rock formation including the region a mile north of Oroville represents a highly metamorphosed series of basic rocks which have yielded amphibolite schists and serpentine. In this formation are included diabase-porphyrites which would readily furnish such specimens as the 'bull's-eyes' described above.

"...Since the presence of diamonds is well established for this part of California, it remains for some one to locate them in the matrix. Just what the nature of that matrix will be is not known. It may not be a typical kimberlite rock and in the form of a volcanic neck, but one of the other great varieties of basic igneous rocks so plentiful in the region. It has not been proved that a kimberlite formation is essential to the occurrence of diamonds, nor that where such a rock exists it must carry diamonds...On the other hand, diamonds occur in a matrix of hornblende-diabase near Inverell, Australia. Since the composition of many of the rocks of the Oroville region is not very unlike this, it may be that the diamonds will some day be found in a matrix of similar type in that region."

Apparently the enthusiasm of the owners of the U.S. Diamond Mining Company was not dampened by this adverse report; in addition to claiming the "blue" pipe, the company acquired worked-out gold-placer ground at the Cherokee mine, where the bulk of the California diamonds had been found. Several diamonds were recovered from these placer workings, in which the U.S. Diamond Mining Company allowed all comers to prospect. On the other hand, no diamonds are known to have been taken from the weathered serpentine the owners hoped was a kimberlite pipe. A shaft was sunk in the area for at least 180 feet, and was open by the time the mine was visited by Mr. Sterrett in May of 1910.

"The writer," wrote Mr. Sterrett, "is ready to hold to the view formerly expressed, that rock formation in the reported diamond pipe near Oroville is practically the same as that in the contiguous country. The portion exposed by the washing off of the overlying placer deposits has been thoroughly decomposed, forming greenish-blue saprolite. In general appearance this saprolite resembles weathered peridotite or kimberlite. Weathering under the porous gravel beds has been extensive, making the complete identification of the rock more difficult. A careful examination of the less altered portions of the 'blue' confirms the opinion that it has resulted from the weathering of basic rocks quite similar to those outcropping along Feather River in the vicinity of Oroville."

The U.S. Diamond Mining Company never mined diamonds. In fact, no one has yet found a California diamond in place, though some claimed to have seen stones with the rock in which they grew still attached to them. One such person was F. F. Barss, who came to California from New York City via Panama and set up in Placerville in the jewelry business in 1852. He, apparently, did as brisk a business in diamond setting as anyone in the Mother Lode; in the seventies and eighties he set five stones in breastpins and two in rings, all of them good diamonds from near Smiths Flat. One stone, according to him, was still clinging to a piece of blue matrix; but where it was from, who found it, and what the blue matrix was, he did not specify.

True kimberlite has not been verified as a California rock, though it may exist here undiscovered; but related rocks — ultrabasic ones and their serpentinized products — are widespread. If they are indeed the source rock of the diamonds, there is ample ground to search. A good way to begin is to investigate the outcrops of ultrabasic and basic rock (serpentine, peridotite, gabbro, and the like) upstream (in either a modern or an ancient stream) from the discovery point of the diamonds. W. H. Storms, writing in the *Mining and Scientific Press* in

1917, called attention to the fact that "in nearly all of the districts of California where diamonds have been discovered, serpentine, or gabbro, or some other kind of rock rich in olivine, or an alteration product of it, occurs in the vicinity where the diamonds have been found, or at some place higher up on the same stream."

A good description of serpentine and related rocks in California was published in the California Division of Mines *Mineral Information Service* in April 1953. An accompanying map shows the distribution of serpentine in California; though it is necessarily on a small scale, larger-scale maps of most of the areas are available.

"The term serpentine," wrote S. J. Rice, the author, "is loosely applied to any of several members of a group of closely related, magnesium-rich minerals. It is also used as a name for rocks composed predominantly of minerals of the serpentine group. Most serpentine rocks are alteration products of peridotites that originally were composed predominantly of silicate minerals rich in magnesium and iron, such as olivine and some pyroxenes. Under subsurface conditions not fully understood, these hard silicate minerals combine with water to form softer serpentine minerals of much different physical character. As peridotite rock bodies are almost always partly serpentinized and as serpentine masses commonly contain some unaltered peridotite, the terms serpentine and peridotite are sometimes used interchangeably.

"Serpentine is one of the most distinctive and widely distributed rocks of central and northern California. Most travelers in these parts are familiar with the characteristic pale green, highly polished serpentine exposed in many road cuts. Equally distinctive are the serpentine terranes with blocks or scattered piles of blocks, which are commonly in sharp contrast to nearby relatively smooth slopes developed on most other rocks with which serpentine is associated. This tendency of serpentine to crop out prominently and to weather to a rusty red color led the early settlers to name many Red Mountains and Red Hills in the Coast Ranges and Sierran foothills.

"Serpentine [is widely distributed] in the Coast Ranges, Klamath Mountains, and foothills of the Sierra Nevada. With the exception of a few outcrops on Santa Catalina Island, no masses of this rock of significant size have been found in California outside of [these regions]. Serpentine usually occurs as elongated masses which tend to be oriented parallel to the regional structure. Individual masses range in outcrop area from less than an acre to more than 100 square miles, and more than 1200 square miles of serpentine outcrops have thus far been mapped in California.

"Peridotites, from which most California serpentines are derived, are medium- to coarse-grained rocks consisting of various proportions of olivine and iron-magnesium-rich pyroxenes. These rocks are given varietal names according to the kind and abundance of minerals in them. A variety composed almost entirely of olivine is called dunite; one with more than 95 percent pyroxene is called pyroxenite. The most common variety contains large amounts of both olivine and the pyroxene enstatite, and is called saxonite. Although saxonite masses are most common, dunite and pyroxenite may occur anywhere within saxonite as irregular bodies. Dikelets of dunite and pyroxenite may cut the saxonite and each other as well.

"Dunite rock surfaces tend to be smooth and even-grained, like a medium-grained sandstone. Saxonite surfaces are similar except that they are sparsely studded with crystals of enstatite an eighth to a quarter of an inch in diameter. Enstatite is recognized by its conspicuous cleavages at right angles to each other. It flashes in the sun, and rock containing a large proportion of it sparkles like a cluster of rhinestones. Pyroxenite is commonly very coarse-grained, and tends to have an exceedingly rough surface.

"Most freshly broken unaltered peridotite has a water-green or yellowish-green glassy appearance. If altered to serpentine, however, the freshly broken rock tends to be greenish-black in color and feltlike or sugary in texture. Even though altered, the enstatite crystals commonly retain their original form, and their softer alteration product, called bastite, looks much like the original pyroxene. Inasmuch as most serpentine minerals are physically weak and tend to deform easily, commonly by shearing, the smooth surfaces often seen on serpentine outcrops are the result of small movements of one surface against another. Wide zones in some serpentine masses have been crushed by faulting, producing innumerable polished slip surfaces that are braided together to form plaits; and these in turn are braided on a larger scale. The slip surfaces curve around scattered blocks of unsheared serpentine. The unsheared material is commonly dark green or black in sharp contrast to the pale green or almost white color of the intensely deformed serpentine. Sheared material may also be honey colored or otherwise light colored, and tends to have a waxy luster and to be translucent."

So far as the host rock for California diamonds is concerned, Mr. Rice concurred with Mr. Storms:

"Although the...diamonds found in California have been limited to placer deposits, they probably originated in peridotite, one of the few environments in which they have been found in place elsewhere. This origin is also indicated by the fact that the distribution of placer deposits in which [they] have been found...coincides approximately with the distribution of serpentine."

Diamonds have been found in or associated with chromite in both British Columbia and Quebec. The chromite in Canada, like that in California, is in serpentine and other ultrabasic rocks.

More than a hundred diamonds have been found in the United States in material brought down from Canada and points north during the great glacial epoch. Some twenty stones, for example, were found in Wisconsin in glacial drift. One of these, called the "Theresa", weighed 21½ carats — larger than any stone found in California. The fact that so many diamonds have been found in the glacial material indicates that a diamond field capable of yielding diamonds of considerable size and high purity may lie hidden in the Canadian bush.

The tremendous continental glaciers that brought these diamonds were probably in existence at the same time as the valley glaciers in California, but they were not contiguous with the California glaciers, and it is highly unlikely that any California stone had its origin in Canada, or that any stone from California found its way to the Midwest.

There is no reason to assume that kimberlite or some other ultrabasic rock is the only source of the California diamonds, though, in view of the geologic environment of other deposits throughout the world, this is the most likely possibility. A few other rock types have contained diamonds, though not many; fine stones have been picked up along the Vaal River in South Africa which some persons think have been derived from diabase and pegmatite in that region, though none have yet been found in place in these rocks. In California, pegmatites— many of them famous for their yield of other gem stones — are widespread, particularly in the southern desert areas; but so far, neither the pegmatites themselves, nor any areas they drain into, are known to be diamond-bearing.

Some authorities point out that the Brazilian deposits contain diamonds in conglomerate beds that have no known relation to ultrabasic rocks; but this fact is of little present value inasmuch as the relation of the conglomerate to any other source rock is likewise unknown.

Some of the more acid igneous rocks have definitely contained diamonds. In South Africa and Australia, diamonds have been found in andesite, an igneous rock containing considerably less iron and magnesium than kimberlite and the ultrabasic rocks. In one area in South America, diamonds are found in highly altered rocks, the original composition of which was andesite or perhaps even less basic material. Sydney H. Ball, in his article on precious stones in the 1949 edition of *Industrial Minerals and Rocks*, published by the American Institute of Mining and Metallurgical Engineers, concluded that "The presence of diamonds in granitic rocks and in some regional or contact-metamorphic rocks is unproved, but is far from impossible. In short, the diamond is a mineral of multiple sources, although kimberlite is so dominant commercially that its importance is usually exaggerated."

There are some scientists who will not allow that a rock can be called kimberlite unless it contains diamonds. Since, even in the richest deposits, diamond makes up only about one part in one hundred million of the rock that is mined, this is a limiting definition.

If one considers kimberlite as a rock type (actually defined as a serpentinized, carbonated mica peridotite) whether or not diamonds are to be found in it, then one finds kimberlite to be rare, but scattered over the world. In the 1950s, in an effort to find sources of diamonds that were not under Western control, Russian geologists mounted an all-out effort to find kimberlite in their own country. They aimed their search at the Siberian platform, where a few diamonds had been picked up. They were outstandingly successful. By 1970, hundreds of kimberlite bodies had been found, and Russia stood second in world diamond production.

The newly discovered Russian kimberlite bodies differ from the South African ones in one striking respect: the cold climate of Siberia does not permit extensive chemical weathering, as does the warmer climate of South Africa; for that reason, the chemically weathered "yellow ground", so typical of African pipes, is missing.

The discovery of so many new bodies of kimberlite – diamond-bearing and otherwise – as well as the invention of methods of commercial synthesis, has reawakened interest in the origin of diamonds and in the origin of kimberlite.

Now that diamonds can be made in the laboratory, it seems clear from experimental results that the pressure within the neck of a volcano could not be great enough for diamonds to have crystallized there.

For diamond is delicate; if heated in an inert atmosphere, it remains diamond to about 1600° C., at which point it turns to graphite. If there is any oxygen present, the diamond converts at a much lower temperature – around 1000° C. On the other hand, it is under very high pressure and temperature that graphite can be made to change to diamond. The conversion of graphite to diamond, even in GE's huge pressure chambers, is quite rapid. Nevertheless, diamond does not always form when it is expected to – when it is in theoretical equilibrium – indicating that there is still much to be learned about diamond.

Also, there is much to be learned about its usual host, kimberlite. In the past score of years, Russian geologists have studied diamond and kimberlite very thoroughly. Their results, as they now interpret them, indicate that diamond is not volcanic at all, but a product of separation of minerals from molten rock deep within the earth. Their arguments are detailed and technical; the interested reader and the serious prospector is referred to the accompanying bibliography for more details. The volume by Elena Frantsesson is of particular value. Not only has Dr. Frantsesson marshalled a thorough argument, but she has also included an extensive bibliography of Russian work on diamonds. Her own book, as cited here, is in English (translated by Professor D. A. Brown of the Australian National University), but most other Russian work has not yet been translated.

There is another possibility which has seldom been considered – at least, in print. This is that some diamonds, and perhaps some of the "pipes," may be the result of meteor falls.

Diamonds have been found within meteorites. After all, it was this fact that gave Henri Moissan his idea for trying to crystallize diamonds in the laboratory. Although Professor Moissan may not have succeeded in creating diamonds from less precious stuff, his name is honored in the mineral "moissanite"; a silica carbide (SiC), a high-pressure mineral genetically associated with diamond, and found in the Russian "pipes." It commonly takes the form of an icicle.

Another high-pressure mineral, coesite, was first discovered as a manufactured product in the laboratory, then found in nature's own high pressure laboratory; in the area surrounding a meteorite fall. It is a form of silica, related to quartz. Small crystals of this rare mineral have been found entombed within diamond — marking diamond crystals as minute high-pressure laboratories in their own right.

There are no records of diamond being found in or near any of the areas in which any of the nineteen meteorites struck that are known to have fallen in California. Some of the meteorites have been lost, except for slices, and the exact point of impact of many of them is not known. However, no concentrated search has been made for meteorites, or, for that matter, for kimberlite bodies, within the state, so this is not conclusive.

The story of diamonds has been a fascinating one, through the centuries. Today, diamonds may provide one of the important keys to the understanding of the story of the earth itself.

HOW TO PROSPECT

There are several possible ways in which to prospect for diamonds in California. One way, and perhaps the one most likely to yield a specimen stone, is to search the places in which diamonds have already been found. These are, chiefly, the hydraulic gold-mining pits on the west slope of the Sierra Nevada. By searching here, one may very well find a stone of respectable size; it is even possible that he may find a diamond field.

A good outfit to take for such prospecting consists of the following items: (1) a pick; (2) a shovel; (3) a sack suitable for carrying gravel to washing facilities. Dr. G. F. Kunz, writing in 1897, suggested a "miner's wallet", a thin bag about four feet eight inches long by one and one-half feet across. Nowadays, when transportation is more readily available, some other container might be more feasible. (4) Two screens, one having a mesh of three-quarters of an inch, the other of one-eighth inch; (5) a small tub for washing; (6) a waterproof tarp or sheet of some sort; (7) a magnifying lens of ten or fifteen power; (8) a set of hardness pencils or wheels; (9) a gold pan.

To examine the gravel for diamonds, fasten the coarser screen above the fine one inside the washing tub. Place the gravel on the upper screen, then shake both screens while they are under water. The coarsest gravel will remain on the upper screen, the medium size on the lower screen, and the smallest material will be passed through both screens into the bottom of the tub. The upper screen may be quickly inspected; the mud and fine sand discarded. The lower screen, on which will rest the finer gravel, should be placed to one side for further inspection. When a sizeable amount has been laid aside, the gravel should be washed in the gold pan. The same method is used as in panning for gold: fill the pan about three-quarters full of gravel to be washed, then submerge it in water; raise the pan to the edge of the water, inclining it slightly away, and move it with a circular motion combined with a slight jerk. This will concentrate the heavier material on the bottom, the lighter on top. Very fine sand should be inspected by means of the hand lens.

If any crystals or fragments are found that are suspected of being diamond, they can be checked in the field with the hardness tester.

Another way to search for diamonds – possibly for a new locality – is to discover the source of those stones that have been found in the beach and river sands. For example, the diamonds found in the Trinity and Smith Rivers might be traced to their source. This might prove to be an alluvial gravel bank, or perhaps the original host rock of the diamonds themselves. One way to prospect these rivers is to use approximately the same sort of outfit described above, testing the gravel in the river bed at regular intervals up-stream, and certainly at the confluence of tributary streams.

In the diamond fields of South Africa, a greased belt is used to concentrate the stones. This is a somewhat more elaborate piece of equipment, and is not ordinarily suitable for mobile prospecting. Because diamonds are not particularly "wettable", they have an affinity for grease not possessed by other stones. When gravel is passed over the grease, the diamonds are caught in it, but most of the other material slips by. Unfortunately, fine silt also will stick to grease, coating it with a film that prevents the grease from coming into contact with the diamonds. To circumvent this, a moving belt is used, so that fresh grease is constantly available. This method was used by the U.S. Bureau of Mines during tests in the Arkansas diamond fields. Four diamonds were used to test the efficacy of the grease; each time the four were thrown into the gravel being prospected, they were caught in the grease, indicating a high degree of efficiency. Unfortunately, no other diamonds were ever caught during the tests.

This method of collecting is not particularly adaptable to alluvial diamonds in gravel beds, as most of the stones pick up a coating of salts during their course down the river, and are thereby rendered "wettable". To change the diamonds to the non-wettable state, the gravel is soaked in a solution of oleic acid and caustic soda. This, in turn, increases the dust content of the gravel, and makes it more important to use a moving belt.

Another method of concentrating alluvial diamonds is by electrostatic separation. This requires elaborate equipment, and is quite unsuitable for prospecting. Details of the process are described in *Gems and Gemology* volume 7, pages 374-375 (Winter Issue), 1953-54.

If the search of the river beds leads to an area that could contain the source rock, or if one wishes to prospect the ultrabasic rocks of the State in hopes of finding diamonds in place, other pieces of equipment should be added. The pick, excellent for gravel, should be replaced by a small sledge of about six pounds, and a small star drill or crowbar. Serpentine and its relatives are very hard, and require considerable effort to break. The broken rock may be further crushed with the sledge and inspected dry at the site, or may be taken to water for fine crushing and washing. Should diamond chips be found in the residue, some method of mining should be devised that will not break the gem quality stones.

Cradle used in separating diamonds in placer deposits, 1870

HOW TO FILE A CLAIM

One may file a claim for diamonds in the same manner in which claims for other minerals are filed. The same general rules apply to diamond claims that apply to all others: "Mining claims", as such, mean claims on public land—that is, on national forest land, unclaimed federal land, and other nationally owned land declared open to prospecting by the United States Government. Mining claims are not valid when staked on private land. Moreover, the prospector who enters private land without permission may legally be prosecuted by the owner of the land. If you wish to prospect on private land, obtain permission.

State-held lands are not open to prospecting unless permission is granted by the State agency in charge.

In general, these lands are open to prospecting in California: all national forests, unless specifically withdrawn; Death Valley National Monument; unclaimed federal land; other federal land, including certain power and water sites, declared open by the federal government.

These lands, in general, are closed: National Parks and Monuments (except Death Valley); State parks, beaches, and forests; federal land held by the military; Indian reservations (unless permission is granted by the Tribe); all private land.

In locating a claim for diamonds, the type of claim filed would depend upon where the gems are found. If your discovery is in gravel or an old stream channel, you will probably file a placer claim; if your discovery is in diamond-bearing bedrock, your claim will be a lode claim.

A great many rules apply to claim filing, though, in general, the process is merely one of placing legal boundary markers on your claim, registering the claim with the county recorder, digging a discovery shaft or doing other specified discovery work, and improving the claim by a specified amount of work each year.

Main street of Cherokee, Butte County

BIBLIOGRAPHY

GENERAL

Ball, Sydney H., "Precious stones", in *Industrial Minerals and Rocks, American Institute of Mining Engineers*, p. 740, 1949.

Hahn, Emily, "Diamond": *The New Yorker*, April 7, pp. 57-91: April 14, pp. 83-101; April 28, pp. 116-132; May 19, pp. 108-124 ; May 26, pp. 94-108; September 22, pp. 99-124; September 29, pp. 39-81, 1956. Published in book form by Doubleday & Company , 1957.

Jahns, Richard H., "The purchase of a gem stone — or what to do until the appraiser arrives": *California Institute of Technology, Engineering and Science Monthly*, February 1955.

Kraus, E. H., and Slawson, C. B., **Gems and Gem Materials,** Mc-Graw-Hill Book Company, New York, 5th edition, 1947.

Kunz, George Frederick, **Gems and Precious Stones of North America,** New York, Dover Publications, Inc., reprint of 2nd edition , 1892, 1968. [Diamonds, pp. 13-38.]

Lenzen, Godehard, **The History of Diamond Production and the Diamond Trade,** English translation by F. Bradley, Basic Books, Ltd., London, 230 pp., 1970. German edition published by Duncker & Humblot, Berlin, 1966.

Liddicoat, R. T. Jr., **Handbook of Gem Identification,** Gemological Institute of America, Los Angeles, 1947.

Sinkankas, John, **Gemstones of North America,** Van Nostrand Reinhold Co., New York, 1959.

Smith, G. F. Herbert, **Gemstones,** revised by F. C. Phillips, 13th edition, revised and reset, Methuen and Co., Ltd., London, 1958.

Spencer, L. J., **A Key to Precious Stones,** Emerson Books, Inc., New York, 1946.

Tolansky, S., **The History and Use of Diamond,** Methuen & Co., London, 166 pp., 1962.

ORIGIN OF DIAMOND

Best, Myron G., and Wilshire, H.G., "Ultramafic inclusions in basaltic and kimberlitic rocks": *Geotimes*, vol. 16, no. 4 (April 1971), pp. 20-21. [Reports on Penrose conference of 1970.]

Frantsesson, E. V., "The petrology of kimberlites." English translation by D. A. Brown: *Australian National University Department of
Geology Publication* no. 150, Canberra, A.C.T., 195 pp., 1970.[First
published in Russian 1969.]

Williams, Alpheus F., **The Genesis of the Diamond,** vols. 1 and 2,
Ernest Benn Ltd., London, 1932.

Wyllie, P. J., editor, **Ultramafic and Related Rocks,** John Wiley and
Sons, New York, 1967. [Chapters 8 and 9 deal with kimberlite. An
extensive bibliography lists many papers on kimberlite bodies throughout the world.]

MINING OF DIAMONDS

Anonymous, "The consolidated diamond mines of South West
Africa Limited," part 1: *Mine and Quarry Engineering,* vol. 21, no. 7,
pp. 266-277, July 1955...part 2...no. 8, pp. 310-317, August 1955.

Gallagher, W. S., "New approach to diamond mining at Kimberley,
South Africa": *The Mining Journal,* London, vol. 245, no. 6254, pp.
9-11, 1955.

Harrison, A. Royden, "Occurrence — mining and recovery of diamonds": *Gems and Gemology,* pp. 154-161, Spring 1952.

Linholm, A.A.L., "Recovery of alluvial diamonds by electrostatic
separation": *Gems and Gemology,* vol. 7, pp. 374-375, 1953-54.

Weavind, R. G., "A process for recovering alluvial diamonds": *Gems
and Gemology,* vol. 7, pp. 365-366, 1953-54.

PROPERTIES OF DIAMOND

Champion, F. C., **Electronic Properties of Diamonds,** Butterworth's,
London, 132 pp., 1963.

Dietrich, Richard V., **Mineral Tables. Hand Specimen Properties of
1500 Minerals,** McGraw Hill, Inc., New York, 1969.

Dyer, H. B., "Physical and mechanical properties" in *Proceedings:
The Industrial Diamond Revolution - A Technical Conference,* Columbus, Ohio, November 13,14,15, Appendix, pp. I-XI. [Includes
bibliography.]

Lonsdale, L., and Milledge, H. J., "X-ray diffraction studies on diamond and some related minerals" in **Physical Properties of Diamond,**
R. Berman, editor, Clarendon Press, Oxford, pp. 12-64, 1965.

FAMOUS DIAMONDS

Dickinson, Joan Younger, **The Book of Diamonds**. Their history and romance from ancient India to modern times, Crown Publishers, New York, 239 pp., 1965.

Shipley, Robert M., **Famous Diamonds of the World**, Gemological Institute of America, 1939; 3rd edition, 62 pp., 1944.

SYNTHETIC DIAMONDS

Anonymous, "Man-made diamond": *Wall Street Journal*, vol. 52, no. 33., pp. 1, 14, 1955.

Bovenkerk, H. P., Bundy, F. P., Hall, H. T., Strong, H. M., and Wentorf, R. H., "Preparation of diamond": *Nature*, vol. 184, no. 4693, pp. 1094-1098, October 10, 1959. [General Electric's experiments in diamond synthesis.]

Brooks, Noah, "The diamond maker of Sacramento": *Overland Monthly*, vol. 1, p. 46-55, 1868.

Cooke, Alistair, "Man-made diamonds": half as big and twice as costly: *Manchester Guardian Weekly*, vol. 72, no. 8, p. 12, January 24 1955.

General Electric Company, "The story of man-made diamonds": *Lapidary Journal*, vol. 9, no. pp. 120-126, June 1955.

Holmes, Ralph J., "Synthetic and other man-made gems": *Foote Prints*, vol. 32, no. 1, pp. 18-25, 1960.

Iron Age, "Materials: made diamonds": *Iron Age*, vol. 177, no. 20 pp. 116-117, May 17, 1956.

Kennedy, J. D., "Man-made industrial diamonds": *American Institute of Mining, Metallurgical and Petroleum Engineers*, preprint 59H57, presented at the Annual Meeting [of the society], San Francisco, February 15-19-1959.

Pough, Frederick H., "Carbon + heat + pressure = diamond!": *Natural History*, vol. 64, no. 6, pp. 288-293, 335-336, June 1955.

Raal, F. A. "Research work at the Diamond Research Laboratory", [Johannesburg, South Africa] in *Proceedings: The Industrial Diamond Revolution - A Technical Conference*, Columbus, Ohio, November 13,14,15,1967, pp. 37-47, 1967.

Van Itallie, John D., "The manufactured diamonds", in *The Industrial Diamond: A Symposium of Technical Papers Published under the*

Sponsorship of Industrial Diamond Association of America, pp. 13-14, 1964.

THE CALIFORNIA DIAMOND FRAUD

Mining and Scientific Press, "The diamond". No. 1: *Mining and Scientific Press,* vol. 25, p. 89...No. 2, p. 97...No. 3,p. 113...No. 4, p. 137...No. 5 [mislabeled 4], pp. 152-153, including map...No. 6, p; 161, 1872.

Mining and Scientific Press, "The diamond fields": *Mining and Scientific Press,* vol. 25, p. 316..."The diamond drift", p. 121...The diamond fields a fraud", p. 344 [Clarence King's report is quoted here]... "The diamond swindle", pp. 377, 380..."The diamond fraud", p. 385, 1872.

Wilkins, James H., editor, **The Great Diamond Hoax and Other Stirring Episodes in the Life of Asbury Harpending, an Epic of Early California,** James H. Barry Co., San Francisco, 1913, Reprinted 1958.

Woodard, Bruce A., **Diamonds in the Salt,** , Pruett Press, Boulder, Colorado, 1967. [Contains an excellent bibliography on the diamond hoax.]

PROSPECTING

Arthur, Edward, **Let's Go Prospecting,** Edward Arthur, P. O. Box 395, Joshua Tree, California, 2nd edition, 1970.

Attwood, Melville, "Hints for diamond prospectors": *Mining and Scientific Press,* vol. 25, no. 11, p. 1, 1872.

Kunz, George F., "Precious stones": *U.S. Geological Survey Annual Report 18 (Mineral Resources of the United States, 1896),* part 5, pp. 1183-1217, 1897. [Prospecting].

Park, Charles F., Jr., and MacDiarmid, Roy A., **Ore Deposits,** W. H. Freeman & Co., San Francisco, 1970. [Especially pp. 76-83.]

[Rice, Salem J.], "Serpentine in California:" *Mineral Information Service,* vol. 6, no. 5, pp. 1-4, April 1953.

Sinkankas, John, **Prospecting for Gemstones and Minerals,** Van Nostrand Reinhold Co., New York, 2nd edition, 1970. [Diamonds , pp. 226-228.]

Stewart, Richard M., 1970, **Legal Guide for California Prospectors and Miners,** California Division of Mines and Geology, Sacramento, 1970.

CALIFORNIA DIAMONDS

1849

Lyman, C. S., "Platinum and diamonds in California": *American Journal of Science*, 2nd series, vol. 8, p. 294, 1849. [First published record of diamonds from California.]

1856

Anonymous, "Discovery of diamonds": *California Mining Journal*, vol. 1, no. 2, p. 13, May 1, 1856. [Tuoloumne County.]

1861

Anonymous, "The great Knight's Ferry diamond": *Hutchings Illustrated California Magazine*, vol. 5, p. 208, July 1860 to June 1861. [Knight's Ferry, Stanislaus County.]

1865

Whitney, J. D., "Geology": *Geological Survey of California*, vol. 1, p. 276, 1865. [Volcano, Amador County.]

1867

Browne, J. R., and Taylor, J. W., "Reports upon the mineral resources of the United States", p. 203, *Government Printing Office*, Washington, D. C. 1867. [Cherokee Flat, Butte County.]

Sillimɛn, Benjamin Jr., "Notice of new localities of diamonds in Californiɛ": *California Academy of Natural Sciences, Proceedings*, vol. 3, pp. 354-355, 1867. [Indian Gulch, Amador County.]

Silliman, Benjamin Jr., "On new localities of diamonds in California": *American Journal of Science*, 2nd series, vol. 44, p. 119, 1867. [Fiddletown, Amador County.]

1870

C.D.V., "California diamonds": *Mining and Scientific Press*, vol. 20, no. 13, p. 194, March 26, 1870. [Fiddletown, Amador County; Cherokee Flat, Butte County; Trinity River, Klamath (now Humboldt) County; French Corral, Nevada County.]

Hanks, H. G.,"Diamonds in California": *Mining and Scientific Press*, vol. 20, no. 11, p. 162, March 12, 1870. [Volcano, Amador County; Klamath-Trinity Rivers.]

Hanks, H. G., "Diamonds in California": *Mining and Scientific Press*, vol. 21, p. 122, August 20, 1870. [Smith River, Del Norte County, Trinity County.]

1871

Anonymous, "Diamonds in Trinity Co., Cal.": *Mining and Scientific Press*, vol. 22, p. 140, March 4, 1871. [Garden Gulch, Trinity County.]

Avery, B. P., "The Trinity diamond": *Overland Monthly*, vol. 6, pp. 525-533, 1871. [General discussion of diamonds, and talk of the possibility of diamonds on the Trinity. Fictional (?) story of the Trinity diamond included.]

1873

California Academy of Sciences [minutes of the meeting]: *California Academy of Sciences of Proceedings* for 1868-1872, vol. 4, p. 196. 1873. [Pescadero Beach, Santa Cruz County; Del Norte County.]

Raymond, R. W., "Have we diamonds in California?": Fourth Annual Report, 1872, *Statistics of Mines and Mining in the States and Territories West of the Rocky Mountains*, pp. 27-28, 1873. [Placerville, El Dorado County: advice to prospectors.]

Silliman, B., "On the probable existence of microscopic diamonds with zircons and topaz, in the sands of hydraulic washings in California": *American Institute of Mining Engineers Transactions*, vol. 1. pp. 371-373, 1873. [Cherokee Flat, Butte County.]

Silliman, B., "Mineralogical notes on Utah, California, and Nevada": *Engineering and Mining Journal*, vol. 17, p. 148, March 11, 1873. [Cherokee Flat, Butte County.]

Silliman, B., "Mineralogical notes on Utah, California, and Nevada": *American Journal of Science*, 3rd series, vol. 6, p. 127, August 1873, [Cherokee Flat, Butte County.]

1875

Raymond, Rossiter W., "Statistics of mines and mining in the states and territories west of the Rocky Mountains; *being the seventh annual report of Rossiter W. Raymond, U. S. Commissioner of Mining Statistics:* 43rd Congress, 2nd session, House Executive Document 177, p. 150, 1875. [Cherokee Flat, Butte County.]

1880

Whitney, J. D., **The Auriferous Gravels of the Sierra Nevada,** Cambridge University Press, John Wilson & Son, 1880. [Cherokee Flat, Butte County; origin of diamonds.]

1882

Hanks, H. G., "Diamonds in California": *California Mining Bureau Report* 2, pp. 241-254, 1882. [Volcano, Amador County.]

1884

Hanks, H. G., "Diamond": *California Mining Bureau Report* 4, pp. 159-172, 1884. [Rancheria, Amador County.]

1887

Kunz, George F., "Precious stones in the United States": *Harper's New Monthly Magazine,* vol. 76, pp. 97-106. [Trinity County; Del Norte County; Cherokee, Butte County.

1888

Anonymous, "California diamonds. One of the products of Butte and Amador Counties": *San Francisco Call,* October 23, 1888. [Volcano, Amador County.]

Irelan, William Jr., *California Mining Bureau Report* 8, pp. 104 - 106, 116, 1888. [Amador County; also contains paper by Henry G. Hanks on California diamonds.]

1889

Anonymous, "California diamonds. An Australian diamond hunter beginning work in Amador": *Globe Democrat,* January 5, 1889. [Dry Creek, Amador County; Cherokee, Butte County.]

1892

Kunz, George Frederick, **Gems and Precious Stones of North America**...2nd edition, republished 1967, Dover Publications, Inc., New York. [Amador, Butte, El Dorado, Nevada, and Trinity.]

1893

Kunz, George F., "Precious stones": *U. S. Geological Survey, Mineral Resources of the United States,* 1892, pp. 758-759, 1893.

1894

Kunz, George F., "Precious stones": *U.S. Geological Survey, Mineral Resources of the United States,* 1893, p. 683, 1894. [Cherokee Flat, Butte County.]

Kunz, George F., "Precious stones": *U. S. Geological Survey Annual Report 16 (Mineral Resources of the United States,* 1894), p. 596, 1894-95. [Cherokee Flat, Butte County.]

1895

Kunz, George F., "Precious stones": *U.S. Geological Survey Annual Report 17 (Mineral Resources of the United States, 1895),* p. 896, 1895-96. [Alpine Creek, Tulare County.]

1896

Crawford, J. J., "Miscellaneous": *California Mining Bureau Report 13,* p. 642, 1896. [El Dorado County.]

1899

Kunz, George Frederick, "Precious stones": *Mineral Resources of The United States, 1898,* part 6, pp. 557-558, 1899.

Kunz, George F., "Precious stones": *U. S. Geological Survey Annual Report 21 [Mineral Resources of the United States,1899],* pp . 422-423, 1899-1900. [Nelson Point, Plumas County.]

Turner, H. W., "The occurrence and origin of diamonds in California": *American Geologist,* vol. 23, pp. 182-191, 1899. [Rancheria, Jackass Gulch, Loafer Hill, Amador County; Oroville, Cherokee Flat, Yankee Hill, Butte County; Smith River, Del Norte County; Placerville, El Dorado County; French Corral, Nevada County; Gopher Hill, Spanish Creek, Plumas County; Trinity River, Trinity County; Alpine Creek, Tulare County.]

1905

Kunz, George F., "Gems, jewelers' materials and ornamental stones of California": *California Mining Bureau Bulletin 37,* pp. 36-44, 1905.

[Indian Gulch, Volcano, Amador County; Cherokee Flat, Yankee Hill, Oroville, Butte County; Placerville, El Dorado County; Nevada County; Forest Hill, Placer County; northern California; formation of diamond.]

1907

Sterrett, Douglas B., "Precious stones": *U. S. Geological Survey, Mineral Resources of the United States*, 1906, pp. 1217-1219, 1907. [U. S. Diamond Mining Company, Butte County.]

1908

Sterrett, Douglas B.,"Precious stones": *U. S. Geological Survey, Mineral Resources of the United States*, 1907, part 2, p. 804, 1908. [U.S. Diamond Mining Company, Butte County.]

1909

Sterrett, Douglas B.,"Precious stones": *U. S. Geological Survey, Mineral Resources of the United States*, 1908, part 2, p. 815, 1909. [U. S. Diamond Mining Company, Butte County.]

1911

Sterrett, Douglas B., "Gems and precious stones": *U. S. Geological Survey, Mineral Resources of the United States*, 1909, part 2, pp. 759-761, 1911. [U. S. Diamond Mining Company, Butte County.]
Sterrett, Douglas B. "Gems and precious stones": *U. S. Geological Survey, Mineral Resources of the United States*, 1910, part 2, pp. 859-860, 1911. [Cherokee Flat, U. S. Diamond Mining Company, Butte County.]

1912

Sterrett, Douglas B., "Gems and precious stones": *U. S. Geological Survey, Mineral Resources of the United States*, 1911, part 2, p. 1047, 1912. [Cherokee Flat, U. S. Diamond Mining Co., Butte County.]

1913

Sterrett, Douglas B., "Gems and precious stones": *U. S. Geological*

Survey, *Mineral Resources of the United States*, 1912, part 2, p. 1040, 1913. [Cherokee Flat, Butte County.]

1914

Anonymous, [El Dorado County]: *Engineering and Mining Journal*, vol. 98, p. 186, 1914. [El Dorado County diamond near Placerville.]

Eakle, Arthur S., "Minerals of California": *California Mining Bureau Bulletin 67*, pp. 7-8, 1914. [Amador, Butte, El Dorado, Fresno, Nevada, Siskiyou, Trinity Counties.]

Sterrett, Douglas B., "Gems and precious stones": *U.S. Geological Survey, Mineral Resources of the United States*, 1913, part 2, p. 665, 1914. [Cherokee Flat, Butte County; Sawpit Flat, Plumas County.]

1916

Evans, Burr, "Diamonds of Smith's Flat": *Engineering and Mining Journal*, vol. 102, pp. 814-815, November 4, 1916. [El Dorado County.]

Merrill, F. J. H., "The counties of San Diego, Imperial": *California Mining Bureau Report 14*, p. 741, 1916. [Imperial County.]

1917

Schaller, Waldemar T., "Gems and precious stones": *U.S. Geological Survey, Mineral Resources of the United States*, 1915, part 2, pp. 848-849, 1917. [Cherokee Flat, Butte County; Smith's Flat, El Dorado County.]

Storms, W. H., "Diamonds in California": *Mining and Scientific Press*, vol. 114, pp. 273-275, 1917.

1918

Mansfield, George C., "History" in *History of Butte County with Biographical Sketches.* Historical Record Company, Los Angeles, pp. 263, 301, 369-370, 1918. [Cherokee, Butte County].

1919

Schaller, Waldemar T., "Gems and precious stones": *U. S. Geologi-*

cal Survey, Mineral Resources of the United States, 1916, part 2 , p. 892, 1919. [Cherokee Flat, Butte County.]

Waring, Clarence A., "Butte County": *California Mining Bureau Report* 15, pp. 181-225, 1919. [Cherokee Flat, Thompson Flat, Butte County.]

1921

Schaller, Waldemar T., "Gems and precious stones": *U. S. Geological Survey, Mineral Resources of the United States,* 1918, part 2, 9, 1921. [Cherokee Flat, Butte County.]

1923

Eakle, Arthur S., "Minerals of California": *California Mining Bureau Bulletin* 91, pp. 7-8, 1923. [Amador, Butte, El Dorado, Imperial Nevada, Siskiyou, Trinity Counties; Fresno County quartz.]

1926

Scott, Winfield, "A diamond quest in California:" *Scientific American,* vol. 134, no. 1, pp. 312-313. [Cherokee, Butte County.]

1928

Bradley, Walter W., "California's commercial non-metallic minerals": *Mining Congress Journal,* vol. 14, no. 9, September, 1928. [Butte, El Dorado, Nevada, Plumas Counties.]

Logan, C. A., "Butte County": *California Mining Bureau Report* 24, p. 177, 1928. [Cherokee Flat, Morris Ravine, Butte County.]

1934

Blank, Eugene W., "Diamond finds in the United States," part III: *Rocks and Minerals,* vol. 9, no. 12, pp. 179-182.

1938

Bradley, Walter W., "California's commercial minerals": *Mining Congress Journal,* vol. 24, no. 9., p. 19, 1938.

Pabst, Adolf, "Minerals of California": *California Division of Mines Bulletin* 113, pp. 15-16, 1938. [Amador, Butte, El Dorado, Fresno, Nevada, Plumas, Siskiyou, Trinity Counties.]

Sperisen, Francis J., "Gem minerals of California": *California Journal of Mines and Geology*, vol. 34, no. 1, pp. 38-40, 1938. [Amador, Butte, Del Norte, El Dorado, Nevada, Plumas, Trinity, and Tulare Counties.]

1948

Murdoch, J., and Webb, R. W., "Minerals of California": *California Division of Mines Bulletin* 136, pp. 129-132, 1948. [Resume; Plymouth, Amador County. The same information appears in subsequent editions of this book.]

1952

Hutton, C. Osborne, "Accessory mineral studies of some California beach sands": *U. S. Atomic Energy Commission*, RMO-981, pp. 41-42, 1952. [Diamonds in beach sands, north central California coast.]

1958

Lenhoff, James, "Oroville's mystery diamonds": *The Feather River Territorial*, Summer 1958, pp. 4-9. [U.S. Diamond Mining Co., Butte County.]

1967

Halverson, Bert, "Diamonds for free — maybe": *Enterprise Record*, Chico, California, September 2, 1967. [Butte County.]

Traywick, Ben, "Diamond dilemma in California": *Desert Magazine*, vol. 30, no. 6, June 1967, pp. 16-17. [Butte County.]

1968

Ekman, A., Parker, I. H., Storms, W. H., Penniman, H. W. and Dittmar, M. E., **Old Mines and Ghost Camps of California**: Frontier Book Co., Fort Davis, Texas, pp. 25,67, 1968. [Butte and El Dorado Counties.]

1970

George, Ward and Vivienne, "Diamonds of Cherokee": *Treasure World*, P. O., Drawer L., Conroe, Texas, p. 60, May 1970.

1971

Rosenhouse, Leo, "Handful of diamonds from the Feather River Mines": *California Today*, August 22, 1971, pp. 18-19, 28. [Cherokee, Butte County.]